Of Life and Motorbikes and Other Stuff

by the same author

The Old Mechanic stories of an old motorcycle mechanic	Burringbah Books 2013
Dominator in the Shadows more stories of an old motorcycle mechanic	Burringbah Books 2014
The Classic Bike Workshop even more stories of an old motorcycle mechanic	Burringbah Books 2015
Classic Bike Dreaming yet more stories of an old motorcycle mechanic	Burringbah Books 2016
Time and Tide the poetry of Peter J. Uren	Burringbah Books 2017
Tommo's Terrific Triumph Trident stories of old motorcycles and their riders	Beautiful Jade Press 2018

Of Life and Motorbikes and Other Stuff

stories old and new, true and not so

Beautiful Jade Press

Copyright Peter J. Uren 2019

Published in Australia
by Beautiful Jade Press
Raymond Terrace, NSW 2324

National Library of Australia Cataloguing-in-Publication entry
Author: Uren, Peter, author.
Title: Of Life and Motorbikes and Other Stuff /
                   Peter Uren.
ISBN: 9781-68969616-6 (paperback)
Dewey Number: A823.4

First Amazon edition September 2019

This book is copyright. Apart from any fair dealing for the purpose of private study, research, criticism or review as permitted under the Copyright Act, no portion of the material contained in this publication may be reproduced by any process without the written permission of the author.

This book is a work of fiction. All characters and events are fictional and any resemblance to real people and events is purely accidental, unless otherwise indicated.

Cover design by the author.
Back cover photograph taken by Glenys Tranter. Used with permission.

Contents

Story	Title	Page
	Introduction	1
1	Time and Space	3
2	The Peter Principle	20
3	Flying	22
4	Geisha	24
5	Grandpa's Shed	31
6	Homeless	35
7	The Rider	37
8	Late Night Drama	39
9	Walter and Rachel	43
10	My Bucket List	53
11	When Reality Bites	55
12	Sea Change	61
13	Obsession	63
14	Philip Island by Muell	72
15	Neither Snow Nor Rain	82
16	The Blade	85
17	Riding Alone	91
18	Going Two-Up	95
19	Once Bitten	98
20	By a Hair's Breadth	102
21	The Adjutant	105
22	Marching to the Beat of a Different Drummer	112
23	136 Hours	115
24	My New Wheels	118
25	Runaway Bay	121
26	A Matter of Trust	145
27	Dressed for the Occasion	147
28	Held Captive	149

29	If Security's the Answer, What's the Question?	161
30	In Love with a Pearl	163
31	Doors	167
32	A Life Revolving	173
33	Which is Best: Two, Three or Four Wheels?	178
34	Why?	181

Introduction

I have not always been able to write. Some probably think I still cannot. I barely scraped through English in my last year of high school. I credit the Air Force for teaching me the basics of good written communication. Still, what is acceptable in formal reports and memoranda does not necessarily make for a very riveting storyline.

    I started writing for myself for two reasons. Firstly, to help me to cope through a very stressful time – my wife's severe illness. I did this mainly through poetry. The second was to share with my friends and acquaintances my motorcycling adventures.

    It was not until I joined Stroud Writers that I started to develop the skills and techniques of a storyteller. Soon after joining the group, they encouraged me to write fiction, something I always had difficulty with. However, within 16 months of joining, I had written and self-published my first novel. It certainly helped that I wrote on a subject I was passionate about, classic British motorcycles. In successive years, I had another four novels and a booklet of poetry to my name.

    But there was more to my repertoire than just writing novels and poetry. I found it just as rewarding as an author to write short stories. Indeed, writing a short story, especially when restrictions are given, like a word limit, using particular words, or writing on a specific subject, has made me much more disciplined, and I find the task much more of a challenge. It is also an opportunity for me to demonstrate that I am more than just a one-trick pony.

I have been collecting these stories for more than a dozen years, but it was not until a friend suggested that I should publish them, that this book came about. I hope you enjoy them.

Peter J. Uren

Time and Space

Part I

I had a fairly ordinary upbringing. I say that because I really did not know much better. I just assumed that all the kids in my class grew up in a family like mine. We lived in a largish house in the mining town of Cessnock. There were five of us in the family: Mum, Dad, my older sister and my younger brother. Mum used to say that my brother had been a mistake, but I actually think that Dad reckoned it was me. As you might have guessed, I really did not get along with my father. Come to think of it, I really did not get along with anyone in my family.

There always seemed to be conflict in our home, and it always seemed to focus in on me. If I was not the alleged perpetrator, then I was the target. But always, I was the one to be punished for whatever supposed wrongdoing I had committed. I used to dread Mum's threat, 'Just you wait till your father gets home.' And, of course, when he did, 'I would cop a fair flogging,' as he used to say, except it was usually about the dogs, the horses or his favourite football team. But the flogging he gave me was never fair.

My father was, what some would say, a man's man (I think he thought he was also a lady's man). He was good looking, intelligent and, in his younger days, quite the sportsman, playing Tennis in the summer months and Rugby League in winter. Recently, he had taken up playing golf. He was also the first in his family to graduate from University. That is how he got to be a mining engineer, and that is how we got to be living in Cessnock, or as the locals called it, Nick-nock. I got the brains from my father, but not his looks or his sporting prowess; that went to my younger brother.

My father was the General Manager at one of the underground coal mines in the Hunter Valley. He was also a gambler and a drinker, though not so much that he wasted his fortnightly pay-packet, or came to notice by the Police, but enough that my floggings (really beltings) with a leather strap usually caused deep welts, across either the back of my legs or my backside. These days he could be brought before the Courts for child abuse, but in those times, it was just the norm. I guess it was the way he was brought up. I cannot imagine that any father would get satisfaction from belting his child; but maybe some do.

I seemed to be the only one in the family to receive these beltings. In my father's eyes, my sister was his little angel, while my younger brother was the apple of his eye, neither of whom could do any wrong. And when my siblings realised that they could tease or hit me with impunity, they did so with relish, and if I did retaliate, I would be the one to be punished. Mum seemed to be scared of my Dad, so she rarely, if ever, came to my aid. But maybe she thought that it was either me or her, and she selfishly decided to protect herself.

School seemed to be the only place where I could be myself. At least it was when I was in Primary School where I had some loving and caring teachers. But when I reached High School, things changed. While I could keep up with my peers academically, physically, I was being left far behind. Where most everyone else was reaching puberty at 13 or 14 years of age, my voice did not break until I was nearing my 17th birthday. What is more, at 15, I was about 30 cm shorter than the average boys of my age. So, I was an easy target for the school bullies; in fact, I was bullied mercilessly. Furthermore, being an emotional child, I was easily brought to tears when I was picked on, which was nearly every day. To make matters worse, I would get no relief from the teachers (who usually turned a blind eye) or my parents (my father called me a sissy).

I hated my family, I hated the beltings, I hated school, I hated the bullies and I hated my life. But what could I do? I could run away from home, but where to, and how? I had no money or friends, and if I ran to my grandparents or other relatives, even if I knew how to get there, they would simply call my father, and then there would be hell to pay. I could always hitchhike somewhere, but there was always the danger of being picked up by some pervert. I thought about killing myself, but even then, they would have won. I felt trapped.

As I mentioned earlier, we lived in a large house in Cessnock. When I say large, I mean it was the largest house in the street. While modest when compared to houses of today, it was large then, being constructed of brick and tile, it was double-storey, had four bedrooms, two bathrooms and a double garage. In contrast, most other houses in the street were single storey, of weatherboard or fibre-cement construction with a corrugated iron roof, had three bedrooms and a single bathroom, as well as a single garage, if they had one at all.

While I was generally free to roam the streets of the neighbourhood, there were restrictions about where I could go and with whom I could speak. At the top of the list, I was barred from speaking to the proverbial "dirty old man in a panel-van". But next on the list was the couple at number 29 on our street. Not only was the lady who lived there of Aboriginal descent, but Dad said they were Communists.

I did not really know what a Communist was, but they must have been really bad people. I had heard about the "yellow peril", the "domino effect" and "reds under the bed", and that they were all somehow caused by the Communists, although I was not really sure how or what they all meant.

On the other hand, the colour of someone's skin did not bother me much, after all it was not as if she had had a choice to be born Aboriginal. In fact, rather than being a negative, I was soon to learn that the lady actually saw it in a positive light. Anyway, there were kids in my school from all different backgrounds. Besides British, there were Finns, Germans, Italians, Greeks, Turks and Lebanese. Some of the Turkish and Lebanese kids were no less dark skinned than the Aboriginal lady at number 29. Even my skin turned dark after a summer of sunbaking by the local pool. Nevertheless, a ban is a ban, and I was not going to break it for fear of receiving another belting.

But things were about to change. The Easter Holiday break was about to end and I was feeling pretty miserable, despite the warm, sunny, autumnal weather. I was headed back to school tomorrow. While I did not worry that I had Math and Chemistry tests in the morning, I was worried that the bullying would resume in earnest. As I wandered, I was not really thinking about where I was, except that I was heading in the general direction of home. I suppose I was daydreaming about how different life would be if I had superpowers or something, when I heard a voice.

'Hello boy.'

I was startled out of my dreaming. I was standing in front of number 29, and the Aboriginal lady had been watering her front garden as I approached.

'I ... I ... I'm not supposed to talk to you,' I stammered.

Ignoring my statement, she asked, 'What's your name boy?'

'Sam.'

'So why can't you talk to me Sam? I'm not a Warrigal, I won't bite; and I'm not a witch, I won't turn you into a toad.'

'But you're Aboriginal, ... and a Communist, ... and my

Dad said I wasn't allowed to talk to you.'

'Oh, I see. Do you know what a Communist is?'

'No, not really. But I know what an Aboriginal is.'

'And what's that?'

'Your ancestors first came to Australia tens of thousands of years ago. So, they were the first people to settle here.'

The lady seemed quite friendly and kind, gentle even. I was in two minds about whether to stay and talk, or run for my life.

'If that's true, that we were the first people here, then why can't you talk to me?'

'It's just that my Dad said so, and if I get caught, he'll give me another belting.'

'How many beltings have you had?'

'I don't know, … dozens, … hundreds maybe.'

'Are you scared of him?'

I thought for a moment. 'No! I'm terrified.'

Suddenly, she turned about and headed toward her front door. Over her shoulder she called, 'Don't leave.'

I was getting nervous. I looked up and down the street, half expecting to see surveillance cameras trained on number 29, or my siblings hiding behind a bushy shrub, spying on me, getting ready to dob me in to my parents.

The Aboriginal lady returned in less than a minute. In her hand was a fur covered pouch with a leather drawstring around the neck. She opened the pouch and produced a small, black, shiny stone. It was maybe 50 mm long and about 20 mm high, in the shape of an elongated pyramid with rounded edges.

'Keep this stone in the bag and in your pocket. It's magic; it will protect you. And you can come and visit me whenever you like. Now, you'd best be going.'

'Thankyou … um, I don't know your name.'

'You can call me Aunty Pearl.'

Before I could say anything more, she was gone. As I hurried home, I began to think about the stone in my pocket. I did not believe in magic. I had heard that some people trusted in good luck charms like rabbit's feet or four-leaf clovers, but I thought that they were all just hocus-pocus nonsense. So, I did not give much credence to their value. I considered myself reasonably intelligent, and I believed in science, so I certainly had no time for magic, or luck for that matter, good, bad or otherwise. But for some strange reason, I trusted what Aunty Pearl told me. I believed that, somehow, it *was* magic and would protect me; but how and from what, I was not sure. I did not have to wait long to find out.

I entered the house quietly via the backdoor. Mum was in the kitchen preparing dinner. I tried to pass through into the hallway to get to my bedroom, but to my surprise, she greeted me cheerily and then asked me if I would set the table. She asked! She had never asked before. But things got better when my sister came out of her bedroom and asked if she help me. I almost fell over.

Dad came home from work at about 5:30; dinner was at six, usually after I had received a belting for my latest misdemeanour. But this time, he came into the house, ruffled my hair and asked me, 'How was your day champ?'

I thought I was dreaming. I thought I must have fallen asleep on the grass in the park in the warm autumn sunshine and that I would soon wake up. But I had not, and I did not. It was all real. I felt for the stone in my pocket – it was there. Maybe it worked after all; or maybe not. The proof would be at school tomorrow.

After dinner and I had completed my chores, I went to my room, ostensibly to study some more for my tests in the morning. But I could not wait to take the stone from its pouch.

I examined it closely. It was black and shiny, but not such that I could see my reflection in it. In fact, light did not seem to reflect from its surface at all. Peering closely, I noticed that there was a tiny pinhole at the sharpest end. It was so small that I doubted a piece of string could be threaded through. But anyway, Aunty Pearl had told me to keep it in its pouch, not on a string around my neck.

I hardly slept that night. I was actually excited at the prospect of going to school. I could not wait to see whether or not there had been any change in how I related to my teachers and especially the class bullies, or rather, how they related to me.

The first day of school term was almost an anticlimax. Nothing happened; and that was a good thing. My teachers treated me just like everyone else in class, and the bullies left me alone. I did not see if they changed their target and began intimidating someone else, but they certainly did nothing to harass me.

The following Sunday, after I had finished my homework, I went for a walk down my street. My Dad was away at Singleton playing golf. I had told Mum that I was headed for the park, although I had no real intention of going there.

I walked past number 29 on the other side of the road. No-one appeared to be at home. I crossed the road and walked past the house in the opposite direction. The house appeared lifeless. I crossed the road twice more and walked up and down the street. On the fifth occasion, Aunty Pearl appeared at the front door. She beckoned to me. I stopped at the gate.

'Did you want to see me?' she asked.
'Yes, but I didn't know if you were at home.'
'Then why didn't you come and knock on the door?'
I shrugged my shoulders, a little embarrassed. 'I, ... um,

'... I don't know.'

In reality, I was not sure whether the ban was still in effect and whether I would be punished for breaking it. Assuming, of course, that my parents found out. Still, I was reluctant to wilfully defy them.

'Are you still scared Sam?' she asked.

'Um, no, not really. It's just that, ... um, ... my Dad, ...'

'Yes, I know he told you not to speak with me, but aren't you doing that right now?'

'Well, ... um, yes.'

'And did anything bad happen to you last time?'

'Ah, no, but ...'

'Do you still have the stone?'

I patted the bulge in my pocket. 'Of course.'

'Did it work?'

'Better that I could have hoped. The beltings have stopped, and so has the bullying at school.'

'Have you told anyone about it?'

'No, of course not.'

'Good, it's best that way.'

'Um, can I ask you a question?'

She smiled. 'You just did.'

'Ah, how does it work?'

'What, the stone?'

'Yeah.'

'Magic.'

'Yes, but what kind of magic?'

'Black fella magic.'

I never did find out how the stone protected me, but neither did I stop carrying it. While the ban on speaking to the residents at number 29 was never formally lifted, that did not stop me from visiting Aunty Pearl and her husband, Stanley, on a semi-regular basis. It turned out that Stanley was a Union Organiser at the coal mine where Dad was General Manager. He said that he was not a Communist, but that his politics were certainly left of my father's.

* * * * *

Part 2

In my last year of high school, news came that there had been a rockfall at the mine where my father was General Manager, and that two men had been killed and another three were missing. One of the missing was Stanley. He had spent months agitating for improvements in mine safety. And, while some concessions had been granted to the United Mineworkers Federation, there were still some unresolved issues. Now, the mine had been shut down and a full-scale mine rescue operation was in place. Dad would probably be away for the rest of the week, or longer.

I had not realised that Stanley was one of those missing – there had been a media blackout – until I dropped in to see Aunty Pearl. There were a couple of cars parked on the street outside the house at number 29, with the sound of mournful singing coming from inside. In response to my knock at the front door, an elderly Aboriginal man came to the door and beckoned me to follow him. We passed the loungeroom which was full of Aboriginal women; that was where the singing emanated. In the kitchen, there were just a few men, all sitting around the table, talking quietly and smoking.

The Aboriginal man turned to me. 'I'm Uncle Robert. You must be Sam. I've heard lots of good things about you.'

I was surprised, not just that he knew my name, but that I had been the subject of discussions.

'What's going on?'

'Stanley.'

Uncle Robert had only to utter his name for me to realise that he was one of those either missing or dead in the mine rockfall. I had a sudden urge to go and find Aunty Pearl and give her a hug, to console and comfort her in her grief. But I did not want to cause offence to any Aboriginal customs or beliefs, so I stayed put.

I sat down at an empty place at the table. Unexpectedly, tears came to my eyes. I felt overwhelmingly sad. Everyone at the table stared at me, but I did not care, everyone grieves differently. Aunty Pearl had no children of her own; Stanley was her only real family. It was then that I realised why she had become so attached to me.

Stanley had two funerals: one at the Cessnock Catholic Church a week after his body had been recovered, and one following Aboriginal custom several weeks later. I was fortunate enough to be able to attend both.

Studies for my Higher School Certificate had kept me mostly occupied over the next few months, so I had not had time to visit Aunty Pearl, except briefly, after the funerals were over. As it turned out, following the period of grieving she had gone away, visiting family in Bourke, Moree, Walgett and Wilcannia. She had returned home before the worst of the summer heat.

'Hello Sam.'

'Hello Aunty Pearl. Did you have a nice holiday?'

'No, not really. There were too many black fellas, too much drinkin', too much cryin' and too much wailin'. I couldn't wait to get back to see you.'

I laughed. 'But weren't they all your relatives?'

'No, some of them were Stanley's too.'

'But I thought he was a white fella.'

Aunty Pearl smiled. 'That's what he wanted all you white fellas to believe, especially your Daddy. He was white when it suited him, and black all the other times.'

A hundred questions popped into my head, but all I could think to say was, 'That cunning old bugger.'

Aunty Pearl smiled, then she became serious. 'So, tell me, how did your exams go? When do you get the results?'

'I think I went okay, but the results don't come out for another couple of weeks.'

'Are you going to the University?'

'Yeah, if I get good enough results.'

'What do you want to study?'

'Dad wants me to do engineering.'

'Yes, but what do *you* want to do?'

'Um, … well, what I really want is to do a double degree in Psychology and Social Work. I want to be a Youth Counsellor, working in the Education Department. I want to do for the kids who're being bullied and harassed, what you did for me.'

'Yes, but I didn't have degrees in Psychology and Social Work.'

'No, but you had something better: the black stone. That was just as good.'

Aunty Pearl smiled again. 'Do you still have it?'

'Of course. I keep it in my pocket all the time.'

'You know you don't need it anymore.'

I suddenly became quite anxious, fearful that Aunty Pearl was going to take the stone from me. 'Won't it continue to work protecting me?'

'You've grown up Sam. You don't need protecting any

longer.'

'But I do.' I was almost pleading, although deep down I knew she was right.

She held out her hand.

Reluctantly, I reached into my pocket and felt the familiar furry bag. I pulled it out and held onto it for several long seconds.

'Come on Sam,' she coaxed, 'give it to me please.'

'Would the stone have protected Stanley if he'd had it on him?' I was stalling for time.

Aunty Pearl thought for a moment. 'No, probably not. I think the black stone protects against people, not things.'

Still she held out her hand. At last I placed the bag in the palm of her right hand. Immediately, she took it away out of my sight and into another room.

When she returned, she could see that I was looking somewhat miserable.

'Besides, if I hadn't taken the black stone from you, I couldn't have given you this. So, cheer up Sam.' She was smiling brightly.

She held out her hand again. In place of the furry bag was a silvery coloured, metallic disk. It was a bit bigger than the size of a 50-cent coin and it had a hole through which was threaded a leather cord. In contrast to the black stone this *was* meant to be worn around the neck.

Sam weighed the disk in his hand. It was much heavier than it looked, about the same weight as a gold medallion of a similar size. But unlike gold, the disk was hard like stainless steel.

'What is it?'

'Don't ask me what it is, ask me what it does.'

'Okay, what does it do?'

'Have you ever wondered what life would be like in a

different place and time?'

'What do you mean? Like in the time of King Arthur and the Knights of the Round Table, or meeting Socrates in Ancient Greece?'

'Yes, or sailing to Australia with the first settlers.'

'What, like with Captain Arthur Phillip and the convicts on the First Fleet in 1778?'

'No, I mean with the first peoples, my ancestors, 60,000 years ago.' She smiled again.

'No, my imagination doesn't stretch that far. But what if it did, how does this disk make it happen?'

'All you need to do is hold the disk in your left hand, close your fingers and then your eyes, and think about a time and a place, and it will take you there. To return to the same time and place, hold the disk in your right hand and think yourself home, and it will bring you back.'

'Really?' I was somewhat incredulous.

'Yes really. But there are some things you have to remember. Firstly, you must return to the same place and time that you left. Don't go from place to place to place. Always come back to your starting place before going somewhere else. Second: the time that you are away is added to your age, even if you return to the exact time and place. So, if you're away for a year say, you will have aged by a year, even though you return to the exact time and place you left. Third: and most important of all, if you meet yourself in a time and place, either forward or backward, don't touch yourself.'

'Why, what will happen?'

'You'll be lost in time and space and you'll never find your way back. And that's the fourth thing: don't lose the disk while you're time travelling. You can imagine why.'

Sam thought for some moments. Eventually he said, 'So this disk is a sort of time machine.'

'That's exactly what it is.'

'Have you used it yourself?'

'I used it recently to say goodbye to Stanley.'

'But why didn't you warn him of the rockfall?'

'Oh, I forgot to mention. That's the final thing: you can't change history, either for good or for bad.'

I thought for a moment. 'That's a pretty powerful tool all the same. Why are you letting me use it?'

'Because I think it will help you to discover your place in time and space, and that you will use that knowledge for good.'

I returned home; my mind was running at a hundred to the dozen. I thought about all the places I could go and everything I could discover. I fanaticised about recovering buried treasure on a tropical island in the Caribbean, or finding my way into the Tower of London to steal the Crown Jewels. But I quickly realised that both of these activities would change history, and they would hardly be for my good, let alone for the good of anyone else. Indeed, even going back and bullying the bullies who bullied me would itself change history. I then deduced that all I could do was to improve my knowledge of the world, and to gain a better understanding about life and myself.

As I pondered the mechanics of time travel, I reckoned that, if I was to age equivalent to the time I was away, then I should be absent only for relatively short periods, at least until I got used to it. To disguise any changes that might occur in my appearance, like beard growth or bumps and scrapes, I would best depart and return at night, in the privacy of my bedroom.

I was excited at the prospect of being able to travel in time and space, but that possibility also daunted me, especially at the prospect of getting lost or worse, something bad happening to me. In spite of all the things to remember and the warnings

Aunty Pearl gave me, I still had lots of unanswered "what if" questions. So, I decided to wait for another 24 hours before my first attempt at travelling through time and space, and then it would only be "baby steps".

The following night, I took the disk in the palm of my left hand, closed my fingers and my eyes, and thought about the maternity ward in the hospital where and when I was born. When I opened my eyes, I could see a much younger version of my father. He looked so proud, boasting to anyone who passed his way that there was his son, me, on the other side of the viewing window.

   I did not want to get too near, just in case, although I was not really sure why. But I was intrigued that my father, who had shown such pride in me at my birth, turned against me as I grew older. I never did find out why, but I did discover that, at least at my birth, he was proud of me. I only stayed in the ward about 10 minutes. I found an empty toilet cubicle (so no-one could see me) and made the return journey from there.

   As I went off to sleep that night, I kept thinking about the reasons for Aunty Pearl giving me the disk. She said it was to discover my place in time and space, and to use that knowledge for good. I would have thought that my time is "now" and my space is "here". But how would I use that knowledge for good? And if my time is not now, how do I discover when my time is? The same goes with locating my space, or should that be place. All this thinking made my head spin.

   I woke the next morning with a clearer understanding of what Aunty Pearl meant. My desire to help kids who were being bullied and harassed was the key. While studying Psychology and Social Work is one pathway to becoming a Youth Counsellor, it was not the only way. And working for the Education Department might be an easier way of helping kids who went to school, a lot of kids, especially those who were homeless and many Aboriginal kids, did not or could not go to school. They needed help even more.

I did not use the disk again. After breakfast, I made my way to number 29. Aunty Pearl seemed surprised to see me. I handed her the disk.

'Have you finished with it already?'

'Yeah, I think so.'

'How many times did you use it?'

'Just the once.'

She raised an eyebrow. 'So, did you discover your place in time and space.'

'I think so. I realised that while studying Psychology and Social Work might be the means to a comfortable end working in the Education Department, that's not where the greatest need is. I want to be able to help kids, from all backgrounds, to discover what you helped me to achieve.'

Aunty Pearl smiled, then she broke out into a chuckle.

'What's so funny?'

'Sorry Sam, but I have a confession to make.'

'What's that?'

'The black stone and the silver disk.'

'What about them?'

'There's nothing magical about them.'

'But there is,' I protested, 'They worked, just like they were supposed to.'

'Sam, they worked because you desperately wanted them to. There's no such thing as time travel, except in our dreams. And the protection from the black stone was you having more confidence in yourself. People just responded to your own assertiveness. Sure, the stone and the disk have been handed down by my ancestors, and they do play a part in our ceremonies, but there's nothing particularly magical about them, except that vulnerable people like you believe in them.'

'You mean gullible people like me.'

'Don't be too hard on yourself Sam. I just saw your need and helped you to find a solution.'

At first, I felt deceived. But then I realised the wisdom of dear old Aunty Pearl.

The Peter Principle

The Peter Principle states that "people are promoted to the level of their incompetence". As I pondered this Principle, having a preponderance for pondering, I began to wonder how it related to motorcycle riding. You see motorcycle riding is one of life's most pleasurable pastimes. There is nothing more enjoyable than riding a motorcycle on a warm, calm, sunny day. In fact, the only pastime that would even come close on a warm, calm, sunny day would be enjoying an oak-aged red with some fine cheese on a picnic blanket with… Well, you get the picture.

Where was I? Oh yes, the Peter Principle and its relationship to motorcycling. Well, I would like to suggest that, in accordance with the Peter Principle, people ride to the level of their incompetence. There has been much said about motorcycle safety and about riders riding said motorcycles within, to and beyond the capability of individual machines. There has also been much written about rider training, capacity limits, speed limits and power to weight restrictions. Finally, and most appropriately, there has been much discussion about attitudes, both of motorcycle riders and motor vehicle drivers in general. However, despite all of the above, and taking into consideration all aspects of the foregoing, motorcyclists continue crash, and many die as a result.

Of course, we motorcyclists would decry the notion that we ride beyond the level of our competence, and so we are quick to blame other factors. And indeed, other factors do come into the equation, especially in collisions involving other motor vehicles. But at the end of the day, it all comes down to competence, or lack thereof, that determines whether or not we survive to ride another day. Yet, despite our individual levels of competence, I would argue that motorcyclists tend to ride beyond that level and into the realms of incompetence. Therefore, it is not how good we are that determines whether we survive the ride, but how good we are at knowing where to draw the line.

A case in point, I went for a ride on Sunday. Last Sunday was a beautiful day, in fact, as I alluded to at the beginning of this article, it was a warm, calm and sunny day. I have a large capacity European motorcycle designed for comfortable, high speed, long-distance touring. And I was riding it as it was designed. However, I undertook an action that involved four other vehicles, that, in hindsight, was fraught with danger and could have ended in tragedy. In other words, it could have killed me. While I don't particularly want to go into the details of said action, what it demonstrated was that I was prepared to ride my bike beyond my level of competence and into the realms of incompetence. I was just fortunate that my action did little more than scare the proverbial crap out of me and gave me an experience about which to write. But it could have been… well let's just say I would never have written this or anything else again.

Like most people, I would consider myself a competent rider. Whilst I have not undergone formal rider training, I think I am as good as most, better than many, not as good as others. While everyone would probably consider themselves to be above average, I'm happy with the average tag. But average, below or above, experienced or novice, it is the level of competence and knowing where that level is that is of utmost importance. Please do not let the Peter Principle of motorcycling apply to you as it did to me.

Flying

Have you ever flown? No, not in an aeroplane or anything like that, I mean real flying – like a bird, only without any wings. I'd look really stupid with wings, like an angel in jeans and tee shirt, and without the halo. No, I mean flying – no superhero suit, no wings, just escaping gravity and flying.

I have. Flown, I mean. Yes really.

Gravity no longer has any hold on me. It's still there, gravity I mean, it just doesn't work on me, unless I want it to. We couldn't have everything just floating off in to space now, could we? But when I want, I just break free of gravity's grasp and fly. Fast or slow, high or low, flying is one of life's great pleasures.

Free from the heaviness that comes from being bound to the earth, I can just float along. While my feet may seem to be touching the ground, that's just so that I don't unnerve people. But when I want, I just go – floating over the earth, gliding over the trees, soaring with the updraughts, diving and swooping like a bird. There is nothing else that approaches the exhilaration of flying. It's an amazing feeling.

Flying is like swimming in the air. To move around I either push off objects or I just think about what I want to do and where I want to go, and I just do it. I set my mind to fly, and I do it. A bit like Superman[1] really, but without the superhuman stuff that goes with it – no bending steel with bare hands, no faster than a speeding bullet, no x-ray vision and no heat rays – just the bit about being able to leap tall buildings with a single

---

[1] I suppose it's more like Peter Pan than Superman, but everyone knows that Peter Pan is for kids. After all, who believes in fairies?

bound. Except I don't need to bound, just take a step. In fact, I don't even have to do that; I can just float off.

The good thing is, I also don't have to worry about kryptonite. But I do have to be careful about flying into things. I mean, flying headlong into a brick wall hurts. And if I land too heavily, I could still break my leg. No, just like flying an aeroplane, landing safely is one of the first skills that you have to master when you learn to fly.

I can go faster by just concentrating on it; slowing down is the same, but it's a bit trickier. If I've gained too much momentum, and I need to wash off speed rapidly, I swoop down and then as I pull out of my dive, I reinvoke gravity and hopefully, if I've calculated things correctly, they should cancel each other out and I land safely. Soft landings are best, and if that can't be achieved by slow speed, then a springy mattress or trampoline comes in handy.

I wish I could take my friends flying, but it's not something that can be shared; it's not like a flying carpet. No, you can either fly, or you can't. If you can fly, I'd love to hear from you – we could share experiences or maybe go for a fly together.

May your skies be bright and your landings safe.

Geisha

Life in Japan had been very difficult for the civilian population during the latter years of the Second World War. Not only were there shortages of staples, like rice and fish, the Americans had been creating havoc with their almost daily bombing raids. Vast swathes of the capital had been destroyed in the raids and the subsequent fires. And since the destruction of Hiroshima and Nagasaki, and the capitulation of the military government, the very fabric of Japanese society seemed to have begun to break down. Peacetime seemed little better than the war years had been.

Komiko's father and her older brothers had all enlisted to fight for the Emperor. Hideo Nakajima-san, her father, had been killed fighting the Australians in New Guinea in the early years of the war. Akio, the eldest brother, had been lost with all hands when his ship went down during the Battle of the Coral Sea. Abe had been killed in the jungles of Borneo, while Katsuo, the one closest to her in age, was missing believed killed when his plane was shot down over Formosa.

With no money coming in and four mouths to feed, besides her own, Mrs Nakajima had sold Komiko into, what she thought to be, the traditional world of the geisha. However, the geisha house, located next to a bar in the Tokyo district of Ginza, turned out to be little more than a cleverly disguised brothel, servicing the recently arrived Allied Occupation Forces.

Komiko had already met a number of American GIs. In her opinion, they were ugly, they smelled, and they were hairy, unlike your average Japanese man. What was worse, they all seemed to be full of booze and bad manners. Several of them had treated her roughly, although no worse than the brothel's madam and her fat, balding husband. She had already had to have an abortion, conducted in the back room of the brothel by an old woman who was also the local mid-wife. While abortions were not illegal in Japan, finding a doctor to perform one, let alone a sanitised hospital bed, were nigh on impossible.

Komiko's dream was to get married, settle down and have children. But living, as she was, in the geisha house, providing for the sexual pleasures of the American GIs, her dream was nothing more than a fantasy. She hoped one day to escape the brothel, but while-ever she was under the gaze of the eagled-eyed madam, she knew she could not get very far. And besides, she had nowhere to go. Returning home would bring shame on herself and her family, especially when her mother had been paid to allow her daughter to be trained in the geisha traditions. If only her mother knew what those traditions entailed.

The American base was about a mile down the road from the geisha house. It was a Friday night and the noise from the bar next door was reaching a crescendo as time had just been called. Soon, the drunken soldiers would be knocking on the geisha house door. Komiko looked around the room; there were about a dozen girls, all young, all dressed as she was, in a colourful kimono with an equally colourful sash about the waist. Their hair neatly arranged in the Shimada style, with faces painted white, contrasting with bright red lipstick and dark eye makeup.

There was a brief commotion outside the door before a group of soldiers staggered into the room. Komiko kneeled nervously as she waited to be approached. She could smell them from the opposite side of the room; a combination of stale cigarette smoke, beer and body odour. Even though this had become more or less a regular occurrence, she still felt butterflies in her stomach, and a sudden urge to go to the toilet. She rose discretely and left the room before anyone could say or do anything. When she returned, a man was waiting for her.

John Baker stood out from the other soldiers. He neither drank nor smoked. He went along with the other men from his platoon in order to keep them out of trouble. He was a good soldier who had been offered promotion on several occasions, but each time he had refused as it meant he would no longer be "one of the boys"; not that he was really ever "one of the boys". John had seen Komiko leave the room, and he was waiting for her when she returned. He was about to approach her, but the madam intervened.

'Hello GI Joe. You want geisha girl? You want suk-suk?' As if to explain what she meant, she made a gesture with her closed fist and forefinger.

John was momentarily caught by surprise. 'Yes! No! I mean yes, and no.'

Komiko stood before him, silent, her head bowed, eyes on the floor.

'You want this girl? She ten dollar.'

With the Japanese economy in tatters and the local currency near enough worthless, every transaction in the years after the war was in American dollars. But even so, John knew that ten dollars was a lot of money for a prostitute, even a geisha, although the girl in all likelihood would receive little or nothing for her services.

The madam repeated the question. 'You want this girl? Ten dollar.'

John reached out his hand and lifted Komiko's chin. She momentarily looked in his face before lowering her eyes again.

He spoke gently to her. 'Would like to spend time with me?'

The madam was growing impatient. 'She no speak ingrish. You want? Ten dollar.'

After a few more uncomfortable moments, John pulled his wallet from his back pocket. He retrieved a crisp ten dollar note from a wad of notes and gave it to the madam. She greedily snatched the note from his fingers and turned away, leaving the couple alone. Her job was done. Now it was Komiko's turn.

She bowed deeply before taking John's hand. She turned and led him from the room, through several sliding paper doors, each one closing with a shush and a clap. The sounds of the other GIs in the front room quickly faded away, until there was only the sound of running water. The soldier could not tell where it was coming from.

At last, the geisha stopped and turned toward John, her head again bowed, her eyes fixed on the floor. The room was dimly lit by a candle. It took a few minutes for his eyes to adjust to the gloom. She knelt down and invited the GI to do the same. Komiko started to undo the sash about her waist, but he placed his hand on hers to stop her. Her initial thought was that he wanted to undress her. So, she waited. Her butterflies had returned.

'I don't want to have sex with you,' he explained. 'I just want to talk.'

The geisha lifted her head, although she kept her eyes lowered. 'Don't I please you?' Her lower lip quivered.

'Yes, of course. Hey, I thought you couldn't speak English.'

Komiko smiled, the first time she had done so for many months. 'You are not like the others.'

'Is that good or bad?'

'You are different.'

'I'm still a GI. What's your name?'

The geisha raised her eyes and looked the soldier in the face. 'Komiko,' she said, almost defiantly.

'That's a pretty name.'

Still looking in his face, she asked, 'What's your name, GI?'

Komiko was suddenly embarrassed with her boldness. Her face would have turned red, had it not been painted white. She quickly lowered her eyes again.

John hadn't noticed her embarrassment. 'My name's John, John Baker of Indian Wells, California.'

'Are you married GI John Baker?'

'No, and I don't even have a gal back home, well not any more at least.'

'What happened to her?'

'Her mom sent me a "dear John" letter after she ran off with a sailor.' John suddenly laughed. 'That was probably the best thing she ever did for me.'

Komiko did not understand what John meant, but she was pleased when he laughed. 'You're a funny man GI John Baker.'

John smiled. 'Just call me John, Komiko, just plain John.'

'Would you like some saké, John?'

'Actually, I'd prefer some tea. Saké goes straight to my head. I've still gotta look after the other GIs.'

At the thought of the others, John quickly checked his watch. Since being with Komiko, he had lost track of time. But with still two hours more before he was due back at the camp, he breathed a sigh of relief and relaxed.

Komiko felt strangely attracted to this American GI. Where once she had loathed these hairy, smelly barbarians, she now wished she could be more intimate with this one. She silently turned around and left the room, bowing low as she left. She returned about ten minutes later with all the implements required for the tea ceremony. As she prepared the tea, she silently hatched a plan.

The Japanese tea ceremony is steeped in tradition, with specified utensils and procedures. The ceremony is unlike how Westerners normally drink tea and is as much a performance as it is a custom.

Komiko ritually cleansed each utensil which included the tea bowl, whisk, and tea scoop, in John's presence, in the precise order and using the prescribed motions. On a low table, she placed them in the exact arrangement according to the "Hakobi temae" procedure being performed. When the preparation of the utensils was complete, she began preparing the thick tea which she handed to John to drink.

After John had drained his cup, he suddenly felt a warmth rise from his stomach. He loosened his tie and undid the top button of his shirt. Komiko watched silently as the GI slowly swayed from side to side, his eyes closed. She moved around the table and gently lowered him onto the floor before finishing the unbuttoning of his shirt.

As she knelt before him, admiring his muscled, hairless chest, she became aware of a distant commotion. At first, she did not know who it was or what it was about, but soon she heard the plaintive call of 'Fire!' and the sound of the ringing bells of a fire truck. She tried to rouse John, but he was fast asleep from the drug she had placed in his tea. He was too heavy to carry, so she left him and went searching for help.

Fire had already taken hold of the front half of the timber and paper building. Smoke had filled the remainder of the geisha house. With poor water pressure, the fire fighters faced a near impossible task of dousing the flames.

Komiko returned, coughing from the smoke and gasping

for clean air. Her only chance was to drag the unconscious John to the fish pool located in the garden at the rear of the building and hope that the water would save them both. She dragged him by his trouser leg toward the sliding door. The roaring of the fire could now be heard quite clearly. She slid the door open and continued dragging him across the gravel path. She eased John to the edge of the pool before jumping into the water herself – it was ice cold. She then dragged him in as the room they had just left burst into flame.

John woke with the shock of the cold water on his face. 'What happened? Where am I?'

'You're safe GI John Baker. You're safe with me.'

Grandpa's Shed

Maddie Windsor was strapping her young son into his special car-seat in the back of the family SUV. His squirming around made the task that much more difficult.

'Keep still Scottie,' she commanded.

'It hurts,' he complained. Tears started running down his chubby cheeks.

'Where?'

'Here,' he replied, pointing to his left shoulder where the strap was doubled over.

His mother rectified the problem. 'There, is that better?'

'Yes,' he replied tearily. 'Where're we going?'

'To see your Grandma and Grandpa.'

He didn't particularly like his car-seat as it restricted his movement too much. But Scottie knew that complaining was pointless. Still, he was willing to put up with a little discomfit if it meant he got to see Grandma and Grandpa. At least he had his tablet on which he could play games or watch a movie.

Scottie loved visiting his grandparents; not only did Grandma spoil him rotten with her homemade cookies and treats, but he got to "help" Grandpa in his shed, away from his over-protective mother. He had two sets of grandparents: Nanna and Pop (his mother's parents), and Grandma and Grandpa (his father's parents). He liked Grandma and Grandpa the best.

Steve Windsor's parents lived in the inner western suburb of Ashfield, while he and his young family lived in the Hills District to the north-west of the city of Sydney. On a good day, the drive would take about half an hour, but at peak times it would take an hour or more. Being a Saturday, it was a good day.

Eventually, Steve turned his car into the driveway of his parents' home. Scottie struggled in his seat, but the straps held him tight until his mother unbuckled him. As soon as his feet touched the ground, he took off, up the driveway and onto the front porch. By the time his parents had caught up with him, his Grandma had already opened the front door.

After hugs and kisses all round, the young family followed the old lady into the house; the kitchen was already filled with the aromas of cooking. There were cookies baking in the oven, a large pot of homemade pea and ham soup was on the stove and, cooling on the kitchen bench, were some piping hot loaves of homemade bread. Cooking had always been an important way of Grandma Windsor in keeping her family together.

But Scottie had more important things on his mind. 'Where's Grandpa?'

'Out the back, in the shed.'

She had barely uttered the words when Scottie dashed out the back door and ran as fast as his little legs could take him up the pathway.

'Don't get dirty,' his mother warned. But she was too late, he had already gone.

Steve smiled at his wife. 'Since when has he ever heeded that advice?'

Scottie stopped at the doorway. At the other end of the self-built shed, which was about the size of a small garage, stood an old man hunched over an ancient timber workbench.

'Hi Grandpa!'

The old man turned at the sound. 'Hi there Scottie.'

The young boy ran to his grandfather and hugged his left leg.

'Be careful son, we don't want you getting your nice clean clothes all dirty now, do we? Why don't you climb up on this old stool and watch me?'

Scottie climbed the stool and sat down.

'Be careful you don't fall off.'

'I won't.'

From his perch, he could see everything that his grandfather was working on.

'What're doing Grandpa?'

'Oh, just tinkering.'

"Just tinkering" was the old man's way of describing any work that he did in his shed, whether filing, screwing, drilling, hammering, sanding, polishing or painting; every activity was covered by the one term.

But Scottie knew this, so he continued. 'What are you tinkering with Grandpa?'

The old man smiled. 'There's no getting past you, is there son? Have you started school yet?'

'Mummy says I can go to big school next year?'

'Wow! Next year, aye. You'll be a big boy then.'

'Daddy said I'm a big boy already.'

'I'm sure he's right.'

The old man again turned his attention to his workbench.

Scottie persisted. 'What're doing Grandpa?'

The old man smiled again. 'I'm fixing up this old motorbike. It's a Norton Dominator 500 that I used to ride when I was a young bloke; younger than your daddy.'

Scottie took in the array of corroded engine and cycle parts that were spread out over the surface of the workbench. They did not look much like a motorbike to him.

'Mummy doesn't like motorbikes,' he said at last.

'Is that so?'

'Yes, she calls them "murderbikes".'

'Is that right? Do you know why?'

'No.'

The old man was going to explain to Scottie why his mother was so vehemently against motorcycles, but he realised that now was neither the time nor place to do so. And besides, his grandson was probably too young to understand anyway. Instead he muttered, 'That's a shame.'

When he got a bit older and taller, his Grandma made him his own set of overalls (which were really a cut-down set that his own father used to wear when he was much younger). Scottie loved them, and could not wait for his next visit so that he could really help Grandpa in his shed.

'Can I help Grandpa?'

'Sure son, what would you like to do?'

'I dunno.'

'Can you polish?'

He shrugged his shoulders.

'I'll show you, it's easy.'

The old man showed the young boy how to polish the alloy crankcases of the motor. With each subsequent visit the young boy made to the shed, the Norton Dominator slowly began to take shape. First, the motor and gearbox were assembled, then the frame, swinging arm and forks. But it wasn't until the old man had installed the wheels and the tank that Scottie could see that it really was a motorbike. And so, in time, the old man educated his grandson on the different steps involved in restoring a classic motorcycle.

Over the years a special bond developed between the two that both cherished. As he grew older, finished university, got a job and settled down with a family of his own, the first thing that Scottie built was a shed, just like Grandpa's.

Homeless[i]

The old man shuffled along the pathway through the park pushing a shopping trolley. There were no groceries in his trolley, as much as he would have liked. No, the trolley contained all of his worldly possessions, which was not much. There were a couple of dirty old blankets that he had "borrowed" from a shelter he had stayed at once, several sheets of cardboard to act as a mattress, and an old school case filled with papers he had kept from his previous life. The man was not an alcoholic or addict; he was just homeless.

He shivered from the cold. There was no wind tonight and the temperature was dropping quickly. In all likelihood there would be a frost, so he needed to find a warm place to sleep before they were all taken. The Balaclava Railway Station was his usual haunt, but the police had moved him on the previous evening after complaints from the public. It was not his fault that his clothes smelled.

He emerged from the park onto the corner of Chapel Street and Alma Road. A lady of the night was plying her wares on the footpath. She spun around expectantly at the noise of his trolley, but turned back again before their eyes met. It had been a long time since he had had the pleasure of sleeping with a woman, let alone having sex. He let his mind wander as he imagined what it would be like to snuggle up in bed on a night like this. It would almost be worth the money, he thought, if he had any.

He watched her for a few moments. She had the shortest of short miniskirts, stiletto shoes, fish-net stockings and a faux-fur jacket. Her bleach-blond hair revealed that she needed to redo the roots. She may have once been pretty, but a life of drugs and the rough treatment of her clients, as well as her pimp, had taken their toll. Life on the streets is hard, no matter how you got there. Life on the streets in winter is brutal.

He trudged down Chapel Street, looking in the windows of the trendy boutiques, cafés and restaurants. He was cold, but he was also hungry. He turned down an alleyway beside one particular café. The smells from the kitchen wafted in the air. He rummaged through the garbage bins, looking for some tasty morsel. In one he found an uneaten crumpet. He used to love eating crumpets smothered in golden butter, and dripping with honey. This one was not as good as he remembered, but it was better than nothing.

'What are you doing here?'

The old man jumped, dropping the crumpet in the process. He turned to face his challenger. 'I … I was hungry. I haven't eaten.'

The café owner looked him up and down before she said, 'Well, you'd better come in then and have some dinner.'

'But … but I smell.'

'We all smell dear, just some better than others.'

The Rider

It was still dark when he awoke. The alarm was set for 6:00 am so he had another few minutes before he needed to be up. He snuggled under the doona beside his sweetheart, remembering their love making of the night before. They had been together for seven years now, but since the twins had come along, sex had not been on the menu very much. He thought about suggesting dessert, but decided against waking her as he realised that he should be satisfied with what he had.

Turning off the alarm before it rang, he trotted down to the bathroom where he shaved and dressed. When he entered the kitchen, his wife was already up and had made a start on breakfast.

'Crumpet?' she asked.

'Sure, but I don't think I'll have time,' he replied with a mischievous glint in his eye.

As he wrapped his arms around her, she said, 'Not that kind of crumpet silly.'

'Darn, I thought me luck had changed.'

After breakfast and a kiss from his wife, he left the house. The ice crystals of the frost covered lawn glistened like a jewel in the weak winter sunshine. It was bitterly cold as he trudged down to his shed, the temperature still a couple of degrees below zero. He pulled open the double doors. His car looked inviting, especially on a morning like this, but his wife needed it today. She had to take their children to day-care, and herself to work. He was left to ride his motorcycle, a Triumph Bonneville.

He had all the gear, but on frigid mornings like this, nothing could shield him from the cold as it seeped through the protective layers. He had tried shoving newspaper down his jacket, but it had not helped. He had already started to shiver, and he was not yet even on the bike.

Starting up, he left it to warm on the centre-stand while he donned his balaclava and helmet. The early morning cloudless sky had turned a shade of light blue to match his frigid hands. With numb fingers, he had difficulty doing up the buckle on the helmet strap. He rubbed his hands together and blew on them, trying to get the blood circulating.

Riding slowly down the drive toward the road, brought tears to his eyes from the cold. Closing the visor to protect his eyes was problematic, as it just fogged up. He knew from experience that there was no such thing as an anti-fog visor. Once underway at speed he could close it, but the wind chill factor made it feel colder.

He arrived at work so cold that he could hardly dismount; his fingers were locked in position. After thawing his hands by placing them on the motor, he made his way to the gate.

'I can't understand how you blokes can ride at times like this,' said the guard stamping his feet.

'Riding on mornings like this just makes you appreciate the good days all the more.'

Late Night Drama

I was sitting in my favourite lounge chair watching the late-night movie. The story line wasn't exactly riveting, but it featured my favourite actor of the forties and fifties, Jimmy Stewart. Unexpectedly, I heard a faint knocking at the front door.

Who on earth could that be, this late at night, I thought to myself, as I got up, put on my slippers and went to the front door?

'Who is it?' I asked.

There was a mumbled response as I turned on the front light. I peered through the peephole and saw what looked to be my next-door neighbour. Wondering what the late-night visit could be all about, I opened the door to be confronted, not by my neighbour, but by two masked, hooded thugs, one wielding a machete, the other a baseball bat.

Before I could do anything to stop them, I was bowled over and knocked to the floor. In a dazed state, I tried to get up, only to be pushed back down by a foot planted in my chest.

'Where's ya money?' one of the would-be thieves demanded.

'I don't have any cash in the house,' I lied.

'I saw ya comin outa the bank today,' he said, 'so gimme ya money.'

I tried to think quickly. This low-life thug must have followed me home. Wondering why he didn't accost me on my way, I suddenly remembered that I was walking with my mate, Bill. I wished Bill was here with me now, though he is as old as I am, and just as frail.

'I didn't take any money out of the bank, I was depositing

money into my account,' I replied.

The lies were getting easier as I tried stalling him, though I was shaking with fear. I could see my attacker getting more and more agitated. At that moment I wondered where my wife was. If she was in bed, then surely she must have woken up with all the commotion in the lounge room. I hoped she had locked herself in the bathroom.

'Gimme ya wallet,' he said as he bashed me in the side of my head, as I tried to get up.

I blacked out briefly as one of the thugs disappeared down the hall and out of my sight. In my dazed state I could hear him rummaging through the bedside drawers in our bedroom and the tinkling of glass as the mirror on the dressing-table shattered and my clock-radio on the bedside table disintegrated under the force of his makeshift weapon. Where was my wife, I wondered? In my confusion and pain, I tried to think of where she was. I couldn't remember whether she was at home or not. She must have gone out I surmised. And then I remembered she was with her girlfriends playing Mahjong. Thank God.

I rolled over onto my side trying to get up, but the second thug returned, planting his boot into my midriff, winding me in the process. With the baseball bat held menacingly in his right hand, he bent down and dragged me to my feet, twisting my arm painfully behind my back. I cried out in agony. His mate with the machete threatened to cut off my fingers if I didn't give in to their demands.

'My wallet's under my pillow,' I conceded, 'but it's empty.' Well, it was empty of cash, but it held my licence, credit card, ATM card and Medicare card; damn it.

With his left hand, he cuffed me under my chin and I crumpled to the floor again.

I must have lain unconscious for a few minutes when my

tormenter returned, clearly dissatisfied with what he had found.

'What's ya PIN numbers?' he called out.

'7963,' I replied weakly.

'Youse better not be lyin, or I'm comin' back to kill ya,' his mate said into my ear.

'They're the right numbers.' I lied again, hoping that by the time they'd got to the ATM, the police would be already onto them.

After that, as if suddenly he'd remembered something, he demanded to know where my wife's 'jew'ry box' was.

Thankfully, my wife wears most of her jewellery when she goes out, so I knew it was mostly empty.

'It's on top of the cupboard in the bedroom,' I said, as I tensed for another kick which didn't come, at least not until he returned. By this time, he was really angry after finding the jewellery box bare. But instead of returning to take out his frustration on me, both thugs started destroying the glass display case in the lounge room, shattering all of the antique fine bone china plates and porcelain ornaments that it contained. They proceeded to smash up the television and DVD player, as well as the old hi-fi player. At least they were all insured.

Suddenly, in the distance I heard the faint wail of a police siren. 'Thank God,' I thought, 'someone's heard the commotion and called the police.'

'Quick, let's go,' the machete wielding thug called to his mate.

'Hang on,' he replied, as he turned and smashed his baseball bat across the bridge of my nose. I must have blacked out again, though I could still hear the police siren wailing, getting louder and louder. Everything became quiet again as I passed into unconsciousness, as a small pool of blood oozed from my fractured nose, seeping into the carpet.

I was roused some time later by my wife, as she returned home.

'Get up!' she said, 'It's time for bed.'

I woke up feeling quite groggy, not really comprehending what was happening. I felt my nose which was intact. I looked up at the television; it was showing the credits of the movie that had already finished, puzzled that it was still working. And I was sitting in my favourite lounge chair. Everything was in its place and in order.

My head was sore, but not from any baseball bat. I subsequently noticed the empty port bottle and glass on the coffee table, and it gradually dawned on me that all the late-night drama was merely a bad dream.

Walter and Rachel[ii]

'Private Scott, this bed is yours,' the short burley sergeant told him. 'Put your kitbag in the trunk under your bed and read and sign the ward standing orders.'

'Yes sergeant.' Walter replied weakly, his voice still a little hoarse from the mustard gas he had inhaled in, what seemed an age ago.

'Meals are at 0700, 1200 and 1700 hours in the dining room on the ground floor for those who are ambulatory, which I expect includes you. The Matron does her rounds at 0900 hours, at which time there is a stand-by beds inspection. Is that clear Private Scott?'

'Yes sergeant.'

'Any questions?'

'No sergeant.'

The sergeant eyed the young Australian suspiciously, turned on his heals and quickly strode out of the room, his immaculately polished boots clomping up the hall as he went.

Walter's throat was dry and his side still ached where the shrapnel had sliced right through his arm and into his upper torso. His arm was already on the mend, but every time he coughed or bent to pick up something or turned around, a fresh stab of pain reminded him that he still had some way to go before his recovery meant he could return to the front. Not that he had any great desire to do that; he had already had his fill of adventure since he left home nearly two years before.

Walter had sailed with his Unit on the troop ship HMAT Wandilla, leaving Melbourne on November 9th, 1915, and arriving in Egypt a week before Christmas. His Unit, the 31st Battalion, D Company, 1st AIF, was sent straight into preparing for the push to secure Cairo for the Allies against the Ottoman Turks. Walter was a driver, and it was his job to get the horses, wagons and gun carriages ready for the run south from the port city of Alexandria. After the debacle that was Gallipoli, the Allies were trying to regroup on friendlier shores to defend the strategic Suez Canal against the Turks.

Several months later, Walter was transferred to another Unit, the 13th Field Artillery Brigade, equipped with howitzers, and preparing to move to the battlefields of France. Walter did not mind Egypt; sure it was hot and dry, but so was country Victoria where he grew up. And the people there were very friendly and their hospitality warm. But France was another matter altogether. The country was already war weary and the stalemate that was trench-warfare had changed the landscape from verdant green farmland and forests to a muddy, barbwire strewn, bombed wasteland. It was one of those bombs, filled with mustard gas, that had caused the injuries that saw Walter evacuated, initially to the Army Field Hospital, and then, eventually to England. When it was clear that he was on the road to recovery, he was sent to Chickerell Camp at Weymouth, in the south of England. The Camp, a converted dilapidated two-storey mansion, was a convalescent facility for troops of the AIF.

Walter sat on his bed. In typical Army fashion, the bed was as hard as a board, the mattress probably stuffed with kapok; but at least he had a mattress to sleep on. He remembered with little fondness his time in the trenches near the front at Fromelles in France; there, he would have been lucky to have somewhere dry to sleep, let alone on a mattress. Assuming of course you could sleep, with shells landing at all hours of the day and night, and the screams of the wounded and dying. This bed, by comparison, was pure luxury. And he had a blanket, and clean linen sheets, yes, and even a pillow.

'Would you like a cup of tea sir?'

Walter was roused from his thoughts by a young lady wheeling a tea trolley past the end of his bed. He turned sharply to the question and immediately winced at the pain. She saw him wince and holding his side.

'Sorry,' she said, 'I didn't mean to startle you.'

'That's alright sister, yeah, I'd love a cuppa.'

As she poured the tea into his proffered Army issue pannikin she said, 'I'm not a sister; I'm a Red Cross volunteer. We have to wear these uniforms because this is an Army Camp.'

'Oh, I see,' said Walter.

'Sugar?'

'Yes please miss, two. What's ya name miss?'

The Red Cross volunteer looked at the young Australian soldier and, blushing, siad, 'Rachel Mayne. What's yours?' she asked, her face turning a shade redder than the Red Cross on her breast.

'Walter Scott, but my friends call me Wally.'

Ignoring his forwardness, Rachel asked 'Would you like a biscuit Walter?'

'Yeah, ta,' replied Walter, captivated by the young English woman.

Walter had never shown a lot of interest in girls back home. Sure, he had sisters and cousins, but they did not really count. As a horse breaker, most of the women that he had met were either married to the farmer whose horse he was hired to break in, or else they were old or widowed. Rachel was the prettiest young lady he had ever laid eyes on.

'I have to go now,' said Rachel, as she wheeled her trolley past each of the beds in the room, serving the other convalescing soldiers in turn.

'When will I see you again,' called Walter.

Rachel made no reply, as she turned the corner and disappeared out of sight.

Walter sipped his tea and ate his biscuit in silence, before turning his attention to the Ward Standing Orders. He looked at the clock on the wall at the end of the room above the door which showed that there was still another two hours before dinner. Carefully, he stowed his kitbag in the trunk as the sergeant had instructed, and then leafed through the Standing Orders.

'The usual bull-dust,' he mused as he signed his name as having read and understood the orders and placed them back onto the hook where they belonged. Where they really belonged is the fireplace, he thought.

Walter was already sick of Army life, 'Yes sir, no sir, three bags full sir, stick it up yer Khyber-pass sir.' He kicked off his boots and decided to have a bit of a kip before the evening meal. All the while, he kept thinking of Rachel.

Gee that's a pretty name, he thought; a pretty name for a pretty lady.

The next morning, he was awoken by a whistle that came from somewhere outside. 'What's up?' he asked the man in the next bed from his.

'Roll call, I think,' he replied.

'Do we have to go?'

'Nah, it's only for the Camp staff: the clerks, cooks and bottle-washers.'

'Good,' said Walter, as he turned over to go back to sleep.

'We still have to get up but,' said his companion, 'breakfast is at seven and we have to have our ablutions done before we go down.'

Walter turned back over, again wincing from the pain in his side. He rolled out of his bed, grabbed his shaving kit and towel, and trundled down the hall to a room that contained jugs of lukewarm water next to galvanised buckets for the waste.

'What I wouldn't do for a nice, hot bath,' he said to no-one in particular, as he washed his face and lathered up to shave. There was no mirror, so he had to shave by feel with his safety razor, something that he had become quite adept at. Then, after a breakfast of hot, watery oat porridge and a mug of even hotter, sweet black tea, he went back to his bed to await the arrival of the Matron.

The sergeant was the first to arrive at the door. 'Men, stand fast!' he ordered, as he snapped to attention, saluting as a large, motherly figure eased past him.

'Thankyou sergeant,' she said as she came into the room, glancing at each soldier as she proceeded toward Walter's bed. 'You're the new boy, are you?'

'Yes, ma'am.'

She picked up his medical file that was on a clipboard hung over the end of his bed. She looked up at him and asked him how long it had been since he had been evacuated.

'About six weeks, I think, ma'am.'

'Hmmm. Well, hopefully we'll have you all ship-shape and back to your Unit in no time at all,' she told him.

She did not expect a reply and Walter did not give one, but he hoped she was wrong. He did not want to go back to the trenches as cannon fodder. When he was transferred in Egypt from the 31st, D Company, he had left all of his mates behind. Those he had made friends with at the 13th FAB had all been killed. He was sick to death of death.

After the Matron had left the building, the soldiers were free to use their time writing to their loved ones at home or spending time in the grounds of the Camp until it was time for lunch.

It was fresh in the weak November sunlight. The frost had already thawed, but a cool breeze had sprung up from the south. He grabbed his duffle coat and went for a walk outside, if for no other reason than he wanted to get the lay of the land. And besides, he hoped to see Rachel again. Well, fortune favours the brave, and sure enough Walter saw her in the distance, walking toward him.

'Where's your tea trolley?' he asked.

'Someone else has that job this morning,' Rachel replied.

'What have you got there?'

'Newspapers, books, writing material, envelopes and stamps,' she said, pointing to the wooden box on wheels that she had guided toward him. 'Would you like something to read?'

'No thanks, I never was much good with words 'n stuff. But you can read to me if you like,' he added quickly.

It was a quiet morning and she had already done her rounds, so she agreed and the two of them sat down on the nearby bench. They were able to get out of the breeze, so they were quite comfortable. Rachel took out a copy of the Times and started reading the headlines. Walter, for his part, rolled himself a cigarette while he listened to her voice, captivated by her beauty. They sat there together until the lunch bell rang.

'Oh my goodness,' Rachel exclaimed, 'I'm late; I have to go and help serve the lunch.' With that she jumped up, folded the paper, stowed it in her box and she was gone.

Walter got to his feet and followed her toward the house. He could not move as quickly as she did. His wounds, which he had mostly forgotten about, suddenly reminded him why he was where he was.

Over the subsequent weeks, Walter and Rachel spent more and more time together. Whenever she had some spare time, she would make an excuse to stop by his room to see him, to speak with him, to spend time with him.

Christmas came and went. The celebrations were quite muted. Shortages caused by the war meant that there was no turkey, and the traditional Christmas cake contained little fruit; but at least whisky was not in short supply.

'What are you doing for New Year?' Rachel asked.

'Nothing much,' Walter replied. 'New Year's not a big deal back home; why?'

'My parents are having a quiet celebration at home, and I'd like you to come. Do you think you'll be able to get some ward-leave?'

'No harm trying.'

'And besides,' Rachel went on, 'the next day's my birthday, so you have to come, if you're able.'

'Your birthday's on New Year's?' Walter exclaimed, incredulously. 'Well, I'll do everything I can to get away.'

Walter was able to get three days ward leave, from Sunday to Tuesday. At least having leave on Sunday meant he did not have to go to Church Parade. Walter was not much of a church goer. He never really understood all of the bowing and scraping and all the clouds of incense, much less the priest speaking the mass in Latin.

Rachel lived in a modest little two-storey house in Weymouth with her parents and her siblings. Walter would have to bunk in with her brothers in the loft, which was fine by him. For their part, her brothers thought it was a 'smashing idea' to share space with a soldier fresh from the Western front. The boys spent their first night together asking a hundred questions about the war. And when they had exhausted that subject, they asked Walter about Australia. They were fascinated with tales of bucking brumbies, of kangaroos and guns, of bushrangers and bushfires, of droughts and floods.

'Australia is still a wild place then,' said Mr Mayne. It was more a statement than a question.

'Yeah, but there are great opportunities if you're game,' replied Walter.

'That's sounds to me like you're a bit of a gambler son,' Rachel's father responded. With that, he retired to his bedroom; the conversation was at an end.

New Year's was a wonderful celebration. As the big old clock above the mantelpiece struck midnight, everyone shouted 'Happy New Year' and then joined hands in singing 'Auld Lang Syne.'

Walter then turned to Rachel, kissed her on her cheek and said, 'Happy birthday.'

At that sign, everyone then joined in the singing of 'Happy Birthday to You.' They all went to bed in the wee hours of the morning, exhausted but happy.

Days turned into weeks, and slowly Walter began to regain his strength. His throat was no longer raw, even though he was more susceptible to chest infections as a result of the gassing. The cold of a bitter winter did not help.

News on the war front was grim. The Allies seemed not to be making much headway in the killing-fields of France and Flanders. The German U-boats continued to make it difficult for ships to bring much needed supplies and ammunition to the troops. And news reports that Russia had made a pact with Germany meant the Kaiser's troops could concentrate more on breaking the stalemate in the west.

As the first blossoms of spring began to appear, Walter and

Rachel were walking through the Camp grounds together.

'I'm going to have to leave soon,' he said. 'I'm expecting my orders any day now.'

Rachel did not say anything; she knew this day would come sooner or later.

Then Walter stopped and turned toward her, 'Will you marry me?' he asked impetuously. Before she could say anything, he continued, 'I love you and want to spend the rest of my life with you.'

'But what about the war?' she asked, not knowing what else to say.

'Bugger the war, will you?'

'Yes, but you have to ask father first.'

Mr Mayne had his doubts, but Rachel was a strong-willed girl, like her mother. After questions about his prospects after the war and where they would live, he finally gave his blessing.

Walter and Rachel were married in The Church of St Mary the Virgin, Dorchester, a short distance up the main road from Chickerell Camp on Wednesday April 17th, 1918, two days before he was due to report for duty at the docks at Weymouth for shipping out back to France.

It would be more than six months after they were married before Walter would see his new wife again, and a few months more before they were to board the ship bound for their new home together in Rochester, Victoria.

Life was tough for the young couple; Walter never fully recovered from his war wounds. But they were blessed with four children, three boys and a girl. Two of the boys went to war, like their father, but only one returned. The girl grew up to be my mother, and she is just as strong-willed as her mother and grandmother before her.

I never got to meet Rachel. Sadly, she died before I was

born, and only two months after my parents were married. Walter, or Bibee, as I knew him, lived into his seventies and carried that piece of shrapnel in his body for the rest of his life. He died in 1973.

My Bucket List

Many people have made a Bucket List, you know the list of the things they want to do, and the places they want to see, before they kick the bucket. Sometimes this list contains some of the more fanciful and inconceivable imaginings that people can have, things such as going back in time, flying on the back of a Pegasus, or holidaying on Venus. But usually, it is a list of the more routine and commonplace items, things that many of us have not had the time, or the finances, to do while we worked full-time.

I made up a Bucket List nearly eleven years ago, before I retired, and before the symptoms of my neurological condition first appeared. I called my list the "100 Things I Want to Do Before I Die". My list was of the more mundane variety, and included things like retiring with enough money, flying in a hot-air balloon, climbing the Harbour Bridge, travelling to New Zealand, Canada and the USA, and visiting Uluru. It included a few items related to riding a motorcycle, playing the guitar, personal fitness and the health of my wife. The list also included a couple of items related to my son.

Interestingly, the first item on my list was to "be the best that I can be; and know it". Every other item would be relatively easy to determine whether I had achieved the thing, either doing something or going somewhere. But I am really not sure how I could ever decide whether I had achieved being the best version of myself. Some people I know are lenient judges, while others judge themselves rather harshly. I am squarely in the "could do better" camp, so I would probably never know whether I was the best I could be, let alone acknowledge it.

The last item on my list was to have no regrets. This is one thing that I can probably never achieve unless, of course, I start to rewrite everything to make the list more achievable. You see, many of the items on my Bucket List have been moved to the "too-hard basket" due to the symptoms and/or treatment of my neurological condition. For example, I can no longer ride a motorcycle, so that cancels out three items on my list. Travelling to Uluru is out, let alone climbing the rock. Same goes with the bridge climb. With so many medications to take, and to take with me, overseas travel is problematic. Also problematic is my intention tremor, so the guitar is out too. So, I already regret not being able to achieve all those things I can no longer do, even though it is now beyond my ability to do so.

Before I finish, there is something strange about my list. Even though it is called the "100 Things I Want to Do Before I Die", my list only has 25 items! Now, if I take out those things I can no longer do, as well as those I have already achieved, my list now only contains 12 items, and includes things like getting fitter and losing weight (I should be able to start work on those things straight away). Nevertheless, it must be time to revisit my Bucket List, and add a few more items, maybe including a few of the more fanciful things I would like to do: fly me to the Moon and let me play among the stars, let me see what Spring is like on Jupiter and Mars …

What is on your Bucket List?

When Reality Bites

I have harboured romantic notions about owning an old motorbike for many years, especially a classic British motorcycle. I have owned motorbikes on and off since I left high school; my best mate at school, Aly, actually rode a motorbike to school – a Kawasaki oil burner (two-stroke) café racer – talk about cool! But it was not until I joined the Air Force and received a posting to Butterworth in Malaysia in 1976, that I came into contact with a large number of classic British motorcycles. That was when the romance was kindled.

Butterworth was once a Royal Air Force Station (Malaysia being a former British colony) and there were a plethora of British cars and bikes left behind when Malaysia gained its independence and the Poms moved out. The locals' usual mode of transport was the ubiquitous Honda Cub step-thru scooter, while those who could afford a car drove either small Japanese Toyotas or Datsuns, and the well-to-do Mercedes or Volvos. The Australians who needed a car had a variety to choose from: Fords (Anglias, Consuls, Prefects and Zephyrs), various Hillmans, Jaguars, Sunbeams and TR Triumphs. That left an assortment of large British motorcycles like Ariels, AJSs, BSAs, Matchlesses, Nortons and Triumphs, as well as assorted small Hondas and Suzukis for those who preferred to ride.

I have vivid memories of a big black Norton Atlas ridden by an airman by the name of Tom. It was loud, and it was fast, certainly when compared to the slow speeds on the narrow streets of Butterworth and Penang. I also remember old Triumphs being used off-road on a motocross track that the RAAF Motor Club Butterworth developed at Telok Bahang on

Penang Island. A number of other friends had bikes, but I didn't have a motorcycle licence, so I just bought a car (actually two: a Datsun Bluebird and a Sunbeam Alpine).

It was not until I returned to Australia and settled in Werribee, Victoria in 1980, that my passion for owning a classic British motorcycle really began in earnest (a "classic" usually refers to a machine manufactured between 1945 and 1980). My best mate, Ray, had owned, in Penang, a 1950s Norton Dominator 88 500cc motorbike. Over a glass or two of port, he would tell me stories about the bike that he nicknamed "Charlotte the harlot" because of the number of times it would let him down when he needed it most. I even wrote about this bike in chapter 9 of my first novel, *The Old Mechanic*. This bike, now in pieces, is owned by another friend, Wayne, in Perth.

I eventually obtained my licence to ride and bought a succession of motorcycles, starting with a 250cc Suzuki, graduating to a 750cc Suzuki and then a 900cc Yamaha. I stopped riding for a while in 1988 after I had a serious motorcycle crash.

Then when I moved to Raymond Terrace in the 1989, I started going to a church where one of the men, Don, owned a BSA Gold Star and a Vincent 998cc Rapide, even if they were both in various states of disrepair. I never saw the actual bikes, but I did see some of the parts that he would bring to church – sitting in a back row seat, he would often polish them during the sermon! He delighted in telling me of his exploits riding his machines trying to outwit the local constabulary. Naturally, this just added to the romantic notions I had of owning and riding a classic British motorbike. On a return posting to Butterworth in 1991, I looked around for a suitable bike to purchase and repatriate to Australia, but all of the good ones had already been snapped up. Those that remained were over priced and not worth taking back home, let alone restoring.

I joined a writer's group after I retired. An ex-soldier, Bill, whom I had met through an exercise program for Veterans Affairs' clients, was a keen motorcyclist and a fellow-writer. Many of his stories were about his daring activities riding a Triumph Tiger 650cc in and around the northern suburbs of Sydney in the mid-1960s. Bill was one of the original "Wild Ones" who even spent time locked-up in Long Bay Prison as a consequence. I just loved hearing him retell his adventures and misadventures on two wheels. How he ever survived is a story in itself.

The die was cast when I started writing my first book, which tells the story of an old motorcycle mechanic who takes on an apprentice and, together, they restore a 1959 Norton 500cc ES2. It took the reader right through the process of restoring an old motorcycle, from rebuilding the engine to getting the bike roadworthy. Along the way, they maintained, repaired and serviced many classic British motorbikes. What I did not know about the technicalities of repairing the various motorcycles that I wrote about, I would research on the internet or ask Ray via phone or e-mail.

I was able to write in such a way that a number of reviewers on Amazon were convinced that I was actually a motorcycle mechanic. In reality, I was, and still am, mechanically inept. But the more I wrote in the Old Mechanic series – there are now four books – the more I was convinced, or rather, the more I wanted to believe, that I would be able to care for and maintain a classic British motorcycle.

Modern motorbikes leave little for the home mechanic to look after. With longer service intervals, electronic ignition, fuel injection, sealed bearings, balance shafts and much finer tolerances, other than changing the oil or lubricating the chain, there is almost nothing to do. The last motorbike I owned that had points ignition was my first "big" bike, a Suzuki GSX750. That was also the last bike I ever tried to adjust the "lock-nut-and-screw" tappets. Many newer bikes are now belt driven, even having dispensed with the final drive chain. Every bike I have owned in the past 18 years was sent to the dealer for a service or repair, and the last four machines were either shaft drive or belt drive. Furthermore, every bike I have owned since my second bike was fitted with an electric leg; only my first bike, a little Suzuki A80, was kick start.

But having written so persuasively about servicing, repairing and maintaining a variety of classic British motorcycles, I started to fall under my own spell – after all, how hard could it be? Despite having been warned by Ray and others that owning an old motorbike was a very different proposition to owning something like a modern Yamaha, BMW or Harley Davidson, I had convinced myself that I would be able to look after one. This view was further reinforced when I joined a classic motorcycle club where I was encouraged to get a classic bike. They assured me that if I needed assistance, they would be available to help.

My last bike, wasn't actually a bike at all. Due to my failing health and balance issues, I had swapped two wheels for three. I bought a Can-Am Spyder Roadster with a five speed semi-automatic gearbox. Not only did the Spyder not have a clutch lever, it didn't even have a hand-operated brake – all the braking was undertaken by a pedal under the right foot. So, not only did I have to forget about using my left foot for gear selection and left hand for the clutch, I had to forget about using my right hand to brake, and use *only* my right foot. It took me about two years of concentrated effort to rewire my brain and get everything right.

Several years ago, I started looking around for a suitable classic British motorcycle to purchase. Due to my poor balance, I felt I needed an outfit – a motorbike with a sidecar. While there were any number of classic motorcycles available, the number of outfits was very limited indeed. I had investigated buying a suitable bike and then having a new sidecar fitted, but the overall cost was prohibitive. I eventually settled for a 1957 BSA A10 650cc with a modified Tillbrook sidecar from Mandurah, south of Perth. I was pretty excited when it arrived late one evening. Then reality set in.

Starting a small capacity (80cc) two-stroke single, is a very different proposition to starting a 650cc four-stroke twin, even if the latter machine had relatively low compression. Knowing how much to "tickle" the Amal carburettors was challenging enough. But knowing how to get the piston to the top of its compression stroke, using the decompression lever, and how much throttle was required, was too much of a new trick for this old dog to learn. But starting the BSA was simple compared to actually riding it.

Driving an outfit is a very different proposition to riding a motorcycle, indeed, it is akin to riding the Spyder. But where I had already relearned all the controls for the Spyder, the BSA's controls were different again. With a clutch lever on the left handlebar, the gear selection lever was on the other side, under the right foot. And while it had the brake lever on the right-hand handlebar, the foot-brake lever was also on the other side, under the left foot. It was all counterintuitive. My brain went into overload the first time I tried to ride the outfit on the road. I started off well enough (after I got the thing started), but as I approached the intersection at the bottom of my street, I stabbed down with my right foot thinking BRAKE, but I was actually shifting up a gear or two. So instead of slowing to a stop, I was actually accelerating. The only thing that saved me was that I was still travelling relatively slowly. I turned a sharp left, narrowly missing an approaching car, and stalled it.

When I eventually got the motor running again, I proceeded at a more moderate pace and let the motor slow me down when necessary. With a lot of clutch slipping and judicious use of the handbrake, I made it to my destination. After the bike was fitted with its new rear tyre, it was time to take the old girl home. At the traffic lights, I stalled the motor once more. It took me three changes of lights before I got going again. Thankfully everyone behind me was very patient.

After I got it home, I realised that riding a classic motorcycle was way beyond my capacity to learn quickly, especially when I still owned the Spyder. Going from one machine to the other would overtax my brain trying to remember which side the controls were on. Inevitably, I would pull or push the wrong lever or pedal, the result being a loss of control and a possible collision. And I hadn't even tried to service it yet!

I had so wanted to own and ride a classic British motorcycle. I still have a strong desire to get Ray's old Charlotte the harlot and restore it. I even have a mate close by who recently retired from the RAAF, and now spends some of his time restoring classic Nortons. But having been let down by the reality of actually owning and riding a classic motorbike, the romantic notions have now been replaced by a healthy dose of common sense.

Sea Change

I do not remember exactly when or how it happened. One moment I was dreaming that I was flying and then – well let me tell you what happened, as I recall it.

As I said, I was dreaming about flying: no aeroplane, no wings, no strings, just flying, when I looked down and everything seemed to be fuzzy and indistinct. Initially I thought it was because I was just looking through the bottom bit of my bifocals, but then I realised that I didn't have any spectacles on. I then looked up at the horizon, but it wasn't there – only a hazy, foggy, indistinct murkiness. I could not quite understand what was happening at first. In every direction I turned, it was the same, this greenish grey haze. I then turned my gaze upward. The sky seemed to be shimmering, it was daytime at least, that much I could tell, and the sun was shining. But there seemed to be a ceiling above me where the light was being reflected back.

As my mind tried to process the information that was coming in through my senses, I became aware that I was neither warm nor cool and there was no breeze blowing. I looked down again, but this time to see if I was clothed, but I could not see that close. In fact, while my head could turn from side to side, and to some degree, up and down, I could not see my body. I tried to hold my hands up to my face, and I was horrified to learn that my hands had disappeared, as had my arms. I could still feel something, that moved somewhat, but I could not bring them to the point where I could see them. I then tried to walk, but my legs seemed not to be functioning either. I wondered briefly if I was actually paralysed. I twisted my body and was propelled forward, yet I could not feel my feet, and wiggling my toes produced another unusual sensation, but one that I had not experienced before.

As the strangeness of my body confronted my intelligence, I looked down again and saw that the ground was covered with long flowing grasses. They were swaying in what I thought was a gentle breeze, which ebbed and flowed before my eyes. Between the grasses there were jagged rocks covered with spiky balls, star shaped objects and shells. I then noticed that there were creatures seemingly floating above the ground. As I edged closer, I realised that there was a myriad of these creatures, some large, many small, of every conceivable colour – fish. What were fish doing floating in the air, and what was I doing floating above them? Then the awful horror of my predicament struck me. I was one of them; a fish that is!

But before I could assimilate my current situation, every swimming creature about me darted away as if in panic. I turned quickly to see a pair of gaping jaws rapidly approaching me. I wriggled my body and shot sideways, just out of the reach of the black assassin. The fur of the sea lion brushed past my pectoral fin as it twisted and turned searching out its quarry. Fortunately, for me at least, another poor creature was in its sights. As I stared, the sea lion closed in on its meal. Then the victim was no more and the sea lion faded into the hazy distance. A sense of calm returned to my immediate area.

So, I was a fish, or at least some kind of sea creature. I had difficulty coming to terms with the change. I was still thinking like a human, albeit someone with a warped sense of imagination. At least I thought I was thinking like a human. I mean, how does a fish think? Do they even think? Surely that is what I was doing now! Maybe I only imagined that I was a human, like when I was flying. Or maybe I am only dreaming that I am a fish. If that is the case, I hope I wake up soon before the sea lion catches up with me.

Obsession[iii]

The train was full, as usual. James had boarded with all the other commuters at the inner Western Suburbs Station for the short journey into Central (Sydney). He was fortunate to find a seat, where dozens of others had to stand. He glanced out of the window and noticed a young woman running to reach the door before it closed. Moments later she entered the carriage out of breath. Her eyes quickly scanned the scene and the lack of available seats. She did not notice him.

From his position halfway along the aisle, James watched her. She was very attractive, maybe mid-twenties, clear, flawless skin, deep red shiny lips and dark brown wavy hair. She was wearing a cream coloured blouse and jacket that accentuated her curvaceous figure, and black slacks covering legs that seemed so incredibly long. He started to become aroused as, in his mind, he slowly undressed her. He lifted his briefcase and placed it on his lap to cover his embarrassment.

At the next station, she moved closer to where James was sitting as other commuters joined the crush. She was now so close that he could smell her perfume. He shifted uncomfortably in his seat. He looked at her face, trying to make eye contact. When she eventually turned to face him, she smiled. She looked so incredibly beautiful. He took that as an invitation to speak.

'Would you like a seat?'

She smiled again. 'No thanks, I'm fine.' She turned around to face in the opposite direction.

'I'd like to sit down, if you're offering.'

The request came from an old lady who had been standing behind him. Begrudgingly, he gave up his seat, but at least he would be able to stand next to her. She was quite tall, about the same height as James. She was so close now; her scent was intoxicating.

The train suddenly lurched to a stop as it pulled into the next station. He grabbed the handle of the closest seat as momentum drove everyone in the direction of movement. His arm briefly touched her back.

'Sorry.'

She turned and smiled, but said nothing.

He tried again. 'Off to work?'

She didn't reply to the question.

Many more passengers filled the aisle as the train pulled into Central. A fat businessman positioned himself between him and her. She was already well ahead of him as the fat businessman let other commuters into the aisle. By the time James was off the train and onto the platform, she was already out of sight. He scanned the sea of faces, but she was nowhere to be seen. He wondered where she was headed.

All that day, James could not stop thinking about her. He wondered what her name was, where she worked and where she lived. During his lunch break, he ate his sandwiches in the mall on the off chance that she would pass by. Of course she did not. On the journey home he looked everywhere for her, but she remained elusive. He began to wonder if he would ever see her again.

The following morning he did, and just like before, she was running to catch the commuter train. James watched as she made her way into the crowded carriage. This time she was wearing a skirt and singlet top. Her long legs were just as shapely as he imagined. On this occasion, a young boy nearer the entrance gave up his seat for her. She sat facing backward but toward him, about six rows ahead of where he was. As she sat down, he caught a glimpse of her inner thigh. He was becoming aroused again.

James studied her face as she stared out the window. He thought she must have been a model, or an actor, or something, such was her beauty. Around her long slender neck was a fine gold chain with a single diamond glistening in the morning sunlight. He imagined kissing that neck as he unbuttoned her bra and fondled her pert breasts.

Determined not to let her out of his sight this time, he made his way to the end of the aisle near the door, well before the train had begun its final run into Central. One of the first off the train, he stood back and waited for her to alight. He had hoped to catch her eye again, but she passed him by, seemingly without noticing him.

He followed her down the platform onto the main concourse. She turned and headed toward the escalator, along a corridor and up a flight of stairs onto another crowded platform where more commuters were waiting for a train to take them through the City Circle. James needed to keep as close to her as he dared. While he did not want to lose her, neither did he want to cause her alarm by being too close. She boarded the train and made her way to an empty seat at the end of the carriage nearest the driver, while he stood at the doorway hanging onto a handle from the ceiling. He was determined not to lose her now.

The train passed through Town Hall; passengers got on and off, but she remained seated. She gave no indication that she had noticed him standing at the doorway. As the train slowed for Wynyard Station, she left her seat and made her way to the doorway where he was standing. He watched her, but she did not make eye contact with him, instead keeping her gaze on the door and the platform beyond. He wanted to say something to her, but he could not think what, and besides, no-one spoke on trains.

He followed her onto the platform and up the escalator, not too close, but not too far away. After they emerged into brilliant sunshine on York Street, she turned and started walking toward Martin Place. The crowd had thinned appreciably by now, making it much easier for him to follow, so he kept a more discrete distance. Her strides were long and her hips swayed as she walked. He was getting excited, just watching her. He thought she may have been heading for a café, but she walked past two of the better known ones.

James was about 30 metres behind her when she abruptly turned left into a doorway and disappeared. He picked up his pace, but when he reached the door, he found it closed. There were no markings on the door to indicate what lay behind, and no doorhandle, just a lock. There was not even a number or a letterbox for any mail. He knocked, but it made no sound, as if the door was made of solid metal. It could have been a secret hideout for all he knew or a brothel. He imagined her in a see-through negligee on black satin sheets and smiled lasciviously to himself. After making a mental note of the location of the doorway he headed off to his own workplace; he was late, but not by much.

At lunchtime, he returned to Martin Place to have lunch at the nearby café just up from the doorway, hoping to see her again. But he would be disappointed once more. He returned to work frustrated at not being able to find out more about her: who she was and what she did for a living. He saw her on his way to work each morning over the next few days. Never once did they make eye contact or speak. But each day, his obsession grew.

James purchased a spy camera over the internet and fitted it into the bottom of his briefcase. All he needed to operate it was to place the case on his lap and press a button on the edge of the lid. He used it on each morning over the next week. Once he returned home, he would download the video file onto his computer. He would become excited when he viewed her sitting or standing ahead of him. But he was never satisfied with just pictures.

He had a day off the following Friday. James would use the day to determine when and where she went after leaving Martin Place. He wanted to introduce himself to her and invite her to go out on a date with him. He was so sure that she would say yes; he did not contemplate failure. He had never seen her with anyone else, so he naively assumed she was not in any kind of relationship. His plan was that he would catch his usual train and follow her as before to ensure she went through the same doorway in Martin Place. He would then watch from a strategic location for her to re-emerge and follow her. He fantasised about being on a stakeout and imagined himself as a kind of secret agent waiting to catch the attractive foreign spy. He never imagined that he was doing anything wrong, let alone illegal.

    He would be working undercover that morning and so he dressed casually – jeans, tee-shirt, sloppy joe, baseball cap and sneakers – he looked quite different to how he normally appeared on a work day. To complete the disguise, James wore a pair of dark sunglasses so no one would be able to see who or what he was watching. When she eventually entered the carriage, she gave no indication that she had even recognised him.

    While he was confident that he knew where she was headed, he still made his way to the carriage door well before the train came to a halt at Central. Unencumbered by his briefcase, he was easily able to follow her onto the City Circle train. And just as previously, she alighted at Wynyard Station, before making her way to the unmarked doorway. Now, all he had to do was to wait for her to reappear. He did not have long to wait.

James was halfway through a cup of coffee when she emerged through the doorway, less than an hour after she had disappeared. She looked up and down the street, appearing to be uncertain of where she should go. She looked in his general direction, but gave no indication that she had seen him, let alone recognised him. Abruptly, she turned around and headed toward Pitt Street where she turned right in the direction of the Bridge and Circular Quay.

There were any number of places she could be going, but he kept following her. This cloak-and-dagger operation fed into his spy fantasy, only he now wished that he had thought to arm himself. A Walther PPK 38 calibre pistol, like James Bond used, would have been the perfect weapon, but he did not even have a pocket knife. Maybe next time he would come better prepared.

She seemed to be heading for the Rocks area. Vehicular traffic was getting heavier, but there were relatively few pedestrians at this hour of the morning. Those who were about were slow moving tourists, gawking at the beautiful scenery of Sydney Harbour. The only object of beauty he was interested in was still ahead of him.

Walking past the Museum of Contemporary Art, she turned left into Argyle Street, and right again into Harrington Street. Every time she turned a corner and he lost sight of her, he would momentarily panic for fear of losing her. But he need not have been concerned. He was about half a block behind her when suddenly she stopped outside the Argyle Hotel. She checked her watch as if she was late for an appointment, before she proceeded to enter the establishment through a large glass door.

James started running, not wanting to lose sight of her. He barged through the doors and ran into a pair of tall muscular bouncers barring the way. Before he could apologise, they grabbed him. He tried to call out, but his cry was muffled when one covered his face with an enormous hand. He was picked up like a toy and carried along a hallway to the far end and into a darkened room. Somewhere along the way, he lost his sunglasses. Once inside, he was unceremoniously dumped on the floor. He was about to protest when a size 12 boot knocked the wind out of him.

A bright spotlight was switched on and turned in his direction. He tried to shield his eyes, but he could not see much beyond his immediate surrounds. He was confused, scared and vulnerable. He wondered what a secret agent would do in similar circumstances.

From the edge of darkness, she spoke. 'Who are you and why have you been following me?'

He felt strangely comforted that she was in the room with him. He should not have been.

'Umm, I wanted to meet you, find out where you worked, where you lived.'

'So, who are you?'

'My, my name's J - James ...,' he stammered. He almost said Bond, but instead gave his real name, '... T - Thomas.'

'Well you've met me now, and you know where I work ...'

'But I don't know what you do, or where you live yet.' He felt strangely emboldened the more she spoke.

From the corner of his vision he saw the boot move, so this time he was able to tense his stomach muscles before it landed. But it still hurt.

'That's enough,' she ordered. 'Well, James Thomas, what if I told you I was a foreign spy who lived on a small island in the Bahamas. And these are my trusty henchmen.'

'I knew it!' James grinned enthusiastically.

'Of course, if that were true, you must be an enemy operative, and we will now have to kill you and dispose of your body at the bottom of the harbour.'

'Umm, umm, I … I'm not really the enemy. I … I won't say anything to anyone, I promise.' James felt scared again; he wet himself.

She laughed at his unease. 'Or I might just be a high-class hooker and these gents are my security. Or I might be a solicitor and these men are my clients. Or an under-cover cop, or …'

James was confused once more.

'You see, where I work, what I do and where I live are none of your damn business. If I had wanted to meet you, I would have done so on that first day on the train. But I didn't.'

James' heart sank.

'Don't you think I noticed you following me each morning? Don't you think I noticed you on the train with that dumb expression on your face, staring at me with your briefcase on your lap? I assume you had a camera concealed in the bottom. I hope the pictures were worth it.'

He remained silent.

'I think you're just a sad little pervert James Thomas. I don't ever want to see you again. Is that clear?'

James nodded.

She abruptly left the room with James cowering under the spotlight.

He was found in the early hours of the following morning bleeding, half-naked, bound and gagged in First Fleet Park. He was rushed to St Vincents Hospital where he was operated on for a ruptured spleen. He gave the police a statement but could not give much of a description of his attackers. James never caught that train again, but at least he was cured of his obsession.

Philip Island by Muell

I had made a commitment to George, my near neighbour, and paid for my accommodation and tickets, so I was pretty much obliged to go; although funny enough, I was not really looking forward to the trip. But, committed I was, and so the motorcycle was prepped, the gear packed and it was early to bed for an early start the next morning.

Wednesday dawned bright and fair and it looked to be a good day for riding. I had only ridden the Muell (my Buell Ulysses XB12X) once before with panniers, when I first picked it up new, but I had not ridden it fully loaded before. I found it a little ungainly at first, but pretty soon I got used to the additional weight and soon forgot about it. Being mid-week, the traffic on the freeway was, as usual, crowded, but it was expected, and so we just went with the flow. Being NSW School Holidays, however, the traffic in Sydney was much lighter than usual and we made our way to the M2/7 without any major issues, or so I thought.

Eventually we made it through to Campbelltown where George signalled to stop. He had a problem, or at least his bike (a BMW K1200RS) did. In preparation for the ride, George had a new front tyre and new front brake pads installed. The big brick has power assisted ABS brakes and must go through a system check before start up. A warning light flashes quickly during the check and then slowly until after the front wheel rotates when it goes out if everything is okay. Everything seemed to be okay, until George started using his brakes in traffic. Suddenly the system warning light was flashing and he had no power assistance. Have you ever tried to stop a car with power brakes when the ignition is off? It is nearly impossible.

That was the problem that George was experiencing, only it was intermittent – sometimes he had brakes, sometimes he did not. When he restarted the bike, the system reset itself and he had brakes again. He thought about turning around and going back or going on and riding more carefully. He found that if he used to brake pedal he had brakes for longer (the foot brake is linked to the front disc, operating one disc calliper). We went on.

We took the turn off to Wollongong at the Picton turnoff and headed for the South Coast. Traffic was light and we made good progress. Joining the Princess Highway at the top of Mount Ousley saw my fuel warning light come on. My bike only has a 17.4 litre tank and I had to be careful how far I rode – there is nothing worse than running out of fuel. We reached Albion Park Rail and the first fuel stop about 10.30 am. While the BMW has a larger fuel tank (about 22 litres), it also uses more fuel than the Muell. Nevertheless, we both needed a rest and a drink. George's brakes were still a concern for him, but we motored on nonetheless.

The traffic from Oak Flats, where the Princess Highway became single lane, was a real hindrance to rapid travel. Besides going much slower than we would have liked, it was also quite busy. It was not until after we had passed the Shoalhaven area that we could increase the pace somewhat. Still, every now and then we would catch up with someone in a 4WD towing a caravan or an old dear going to the club to play bingo, doing 60 in a 100 zone – very frustrating. However, the road was very good, winding around the hills and swooping down into valleys of this very picturesque and productive farming country.

We stopped again at Ulladulla for lunch, but we were early and lunch would not be served for another half an hour, so we pressed on rather than wait. We would pass through many more small country towns on our journey down the coast. We eventually stopped for lunch at Moruya at a country pub. As we sat on the front veranda eating our toasted sandwiches and sipping our drinks, we saw a variety of riders on their bikes, loaded with gear headed for the Island. Some were two up, but most of them were riding solo, on every type of bike imaginable: tourers, nakeds, cruisers, and sports, Italian, German, British, American and Japanese. It really made us feel part of a great annual pilgrimage.

The afternoon wore on and we stopped again at Eden for our last fuel stop in NSW before crossing into Victoria and on to our accommodation at Cann River. The road from Eden is excellent, winding through the forests of South-Eastern Australia. But we were tired after a day in the saddle and the sun was low in the western sky making visibility difficult. I was really concerned about hitting a stray wombat or wallaby in the darkening afternoon. To make matters worse, I had a headache, and only wanted to stop and sleep. George took the lead on the road (we took turns leading throughout the trip) and soon we were at Cann River and booking into our rooms. We arrived about 5.00 pm, 11 hours after we had started on the road. Even though we had had plenty of stops for fuel, both for ourselves and our bikes, we were tired and needed a rest. After a counter meal at the pub across the road and a beer or two, it was off to bed, for me and the Muell.

Thursday morning, we were both up early. After a quick wash and feed, we were on the road again just after 7.00 am. The road from Cann River to Orbost was even better than the road from Eden. And I appreciated it even more because I was refreshed from a good night's rest and the sun was at our backs. We made good progress and looked to arrive at our lodgings at Philip Island by early afternoon.

We took on more fuel at Lakes Entrance and then turned off the highway just after Bairnsdale for the back road to Sale. This turned out to be a fateful decision. We took the turn-off to miss the traffic of the highway, as well as keeping away from all the bikes, and accompanying police, taking part in the Barry Sheene memorial ride. After passing the local airport, the road winds its way through the very flat farming land of East Gippsland. We were making good progress, sitting as we were about 10-20 ks above the posted speed limit. About 20 kilometres out of Sale I noticed a warning light appear on my dash. As I puzzled as to what it might mean (my bike still seemed to be going okay), suddenly the instruments stopped working. By now I was more than a little perplexed. I decided to stop my bike in case I was doing more damage than had already been done. This turned out to be the wrong move, because when I stopped the engine, it could not be restarted. It was dead.

By this time, George had disappeared from sight – it would be another ten minutes or so before he realised that there was a problem and returned to where I was stranded by the side of the road. We tried to bump start the bike, but could not get it going. We pushed it into some shade, and then sent out an SOS to the nearest bike shop (Vern Graham Yamaha in Sale) to come and pick me up in his van. The nearest Buell dealer was in Dandenong (about three or more hours away) and a call to the place where I bought my bike was no help. The Workshop Manager, Mitch, immediately set about fixing my bike. He traced the problem to a flat battery, although he suspected that the rectifier may have been playing up. He hooked up a new battery and pretty soon I was on my way again, only to break down again, this time, 20 kilometres the other side of Sale. Another phone call saw the van again picking me, my bike and gear back to the workshop. Meanwhile, George took to the road to make it to Philip Island before it got dark. With accommodation already booked and paid for, it was pointless us both staying in Sale to wait for the Muell to get repaired.

After dropping my bike at the workshop and me to a motel, Mitch was soon on the phone to the nearest Buell dealer to order a new rectifier. Meanwhile, I called my mate, Ray, who also had a Buell Ulysses that, as it turned out, had suffered the same problem. It turned out that the female sockets in the connector, where the rectifier enters the loom (Connector 77), were slightly deformed and had arced to the mating male pins of the voltage regulator, effectively forming a layer of insulation on the pins (an apparent known problem with this model Buell).

Next morning Mitch spoke to my mate and then, following his advice, went about fixing the problem, this time for good. I left Sale again about 10.30 am on Friday morning with a degree of trepidation, hoping that the bike would not let me down again – it didn't. Pretty soon I was well on my way to Philip Island – the bike never missing a beat getting there, and subsequently, all the way back home again. I took a different route to George. I stuck to the highway, passing through Traralgon and Morwell, before turning off onto the Strzelecki Highway and passing through Leongatha and Wonthaggi before the final run to the Island.

The accommodation at Philip Island was great. We were booked into a fully self-contained cottage located on a working dairy farm about three kilometres by road from the track on Philip Island that George had found on the internet. Our hosts were very gracious to us and even offered to drop us off and pick us up each day, morning and afternoon – how good was that! So, even though we had free parking passes for our bikes, they were not needed. More than that, the refrigerator and cupboards were stocked with essentials like orange juice, eggs, bread, tea and sugar, and there was even a bowl of fruit on the table for us.

Even though I had arrived 24 hours later than George, I did not miss too much, except getting wet at the track (I got wet on the road instead). We went out to the track on Saturday morning about 9.30, and set about exploring the place for good vantage points for the race. We also visited the Expo and some of the other exhibits around the track. Then we took in free practice and qualifying for the 125s, 250s and MotoGP bikes. Standing trackside at turn one when the MotoGP bikes were on the track, the sound was incredible, especially from the pneumatic-valve Hondas of Nicky Hayden and Danny Pedrosa. To suggest that they scream does not do them justice – it was truly ear-piercing. I was just thankful that I had remembered to take ear plugs with me. The other thing I noticed was the incredible speed. The top bikes were hitting 320+ kph at the end of the main straight. Seeing these bikes at those speeds on television gives you little understanding of how really fast that is – amazing!

While we were at the track, we were also able to get into the Support paddock where we could get up close and personal to the garages of the bikes and riders on the Support Program. We saw all the current crop of Australian Superbikes and some of the riders, like the Stauffer brothers. I even met one of my heroes from Superbike racing of 30 years ago – Robbie Phyllis; he still rides the same bike he rode then, but now in a class called Forgotten Era.

Sitting trackside during Saturday afternoon, watching practice and qualifying, basking in the mid-Spring sun in the cool breeze blowing off Bass Straight, I did not realise that I was getting sun burned, and boy did I get burned. While I had brought a hat with me, it gave me little protection for my face.

Note to self: get some sun-screen for race day.

We left the track early (before milking started) and got changed to ride into town for dinner and to get some essentials – beer and chocolate, oh and some sun cream. The main town on Philip Island is Cowes and it was jam-packed with bikes – they were everywhere. Half the main street was blocked off to traffic and to allow bike parking in the street. Again, there was every sort of bike you could imagine. We ate fish and chips on the footpath while watching the bikes and people as they paraded past. After eating, we left to get an early night's sleep so that we could get to the track as soon as it opened in the morning to get a track-side position at turn 12.

On Sunday morning we got to the track at just after 7.00 am. The gates opened at 7.30, but even so, we were very fortunate to get a track-side position. We only just squeezed into the last vacant spot on the fence. I kept guard while George went off to the Expo again and for coffee. We would subsequently take turns throughout the day, one guarding our seats and position while the other went out for food, drinks or toilet break.

It was a long day, but it went quickly enough. There was free practice in the morning for the 125s, 250s and MotoGP bikes, as well as some support races – Superbikes and Supersports. We also briefly saw some stunt riders and Randy Mamola pulling wheelies onto the main straight while taking some celebrity on the back of his Ducati. While in the afternoon, we saw the 125, 250 and MotoGP races. It was all terrific, especially Valentino Rossi, the recently crowned 2008 World Champion, coming from 12th on the grid to finish second behind Casey Stoner, the 2007 World Champion, while Nicky Hayden, the 2006 World Champion was third.

As soon as the race was over, we made a beeline for the exit and back to our accommodation. We had another early night (it was becoming a habit by now) for an early start off the Island on Monday morning. The morning did not really dawn – it was more a grey drizzly gloom that had us reaching for our wet-weather gear. It was cold, wet and windy as we made our way off the Island and east. We would not see the sun until we again neared Sale, but it was only a fleeting glimpse. Even though the sun was not making visibility an issue, the cold air was. It was so cold and wet that my visor kept fogging up. When I opened my visor, the rain would wet my glasses, so I had water on the outside and inside. Furthermore, when I opened my visor, the cold air would make my eyes water, making visibility even more difficult.

We had refuelled at Cowes on the Saturday evening, so we did not need to fill up again until Bairnsdale. By then, the rain had stopped and the sun had begun to make a belated appearance. We headed off again and stopped for fuel and food at Cann River – same pub, same meal. As we headed off again (we had decided to go via Bombala and Cooma), the storm clouds were gathering once again. We were fortunate to stay ahead of much of the rain, but the wind was gathering strength. The higher we went into the mountains, and the closer we came to Cooma, the nastier the weather became. The road from Cann River to the top of the Great Dividing Range (1117 metres above sea level) is magic, but as we neared the top, we struggled to stay on the road. When the wind was not dragging on us head-on, it was whipping us from the side with ferocious gusts.

We made it to Cooma about 3.00 pm, just before the weather really closed in. By 4.00 pm, it was snowing, and those who had arrived at the motel after that showed evidence of the cold with ice in their whiskers. Talk about being as cold as a mother-in-law's kiss! We had dinner at the Cooma RSL and I told George then that I wanted to go straight home. When my mind turns to home, I want to get there the quickest way I can, and that was straight up the highway. We had talked about going through Lithgow, the Bells Line of Road and the Putty Road if the weather was kind, but now that home was on my mind, I wanted to go home straight.

We left Cooma about 7.30 am. The forecast was for -3 degrees that morning, and it certainly felt that cold. But at least the wind had dropped somewhat and the clouds had pretty much disappeared. We rode together at a good (legal) pace, heading for Queanbeyan and a refuel. It was just as well that the pace was sedate because we passed a highway patrol car going the other way. I am sure he would have loved to cop a couple of bikes first up in the morning.

We had thawed out by Queanbeyan, and refuelled. It was then that George decided he wanted to find the Canberra BMW dealer to sort out the problem he had been having with his brakes before he hit the Sydney traffic again or the Putty Road corners. So, we parted company and I headed for Goulbourn and home. I refuelled again in Sydney and took the freeway to Raymond Terrace.

I arrived home, tired but happy in the early afternoon. The Muell performed well over the trip, recording extraordinary fuel economy for such a large adventure tourer type bike (on one leg I got 4.55 lt/100 kms or about 62 mpg). And apart from the breakdown near Sale (for which I have already forgiven it) I had no problems on the trip. The Muell was comfortable, had ample power, handled well and took a mountain of gear safely to the Island and back home again. Would I go to the Island again? No, I've ticked that box. But there are certainly more places to go and visit, only next time I'll take the warmer and hopefully drier option.

Thanks go to George for his company throughout most of

the trip, for organising the route and the accommodation and for his help when I broke down. Thanks too to Mitch, the Workshop Manager at Vern Graham Yamaha in Sale for his assistance in getting me going again. Thanks also for my mate Ray; without his expertise and advice, without which I would still be waiting for a part from H-D that still would not have had me on the road.

Neither Snow Nor Rain

The unofficial creed of the United States Postal Service declares: "Neither snow nor rain nor heat nor gloom of night stays these couriers from the swift completion of their appointed rounds."

Like many a dedicated motorcyclist, in my early days of riding, nothing could or would deter me from riding, not least the weather. Whether there was rain, hail, sleet or strong winds, and living as I did in Melbourne, we often had all kinds of weather in just one day, nothing would stop me from riding my motorcycle.

There is a saying in Melbourne: "If you don't like the weather, just wait a few minutes and it will change." So, because of the variability of the weather, a keen rider will dress appropriately. When I commuted from my home at Wyndham Vale in to Victoria Barracks on St Kilda Road, I always wore full protective garb, regardless of the season. I wore either a waxed-cotton suit or leather jacket and pants, touring boots, full-face helmet, balaclava and gloves, and sometimes, mittens, all in black. My boss used to call me Darth Vader!

I loved riding so much. I loved going to work because I could ride my motorbike, and I loved the return journey home because I could ride my bike. I loved riding during the week, and I loved riding on the weekends. I loved riding with my mates, and I loved riding alone, two-up or solo. I even loved riding pillion.

One time, my mate Bill Zacharia called to ask if I wanted to go for a ride down the Great Ocean Road (I did not have a bike at the time). There would be a few of us: Bill, Ray and

Anna, and Andrew (Bill's brother). Bill had a classic Kawasaki Z900, and I would be riding on the back. Naturally, I said yes!

The weather was fine when we left home, but turned cloudy as we passed through Geelong. A light shower started as we rode through Lorne, but nothing could deter us from the joy of motorcycling on the Great Ocean Road. We were riding at a good pace, despite the wet and greasy roads. I just loved being on the back of the Kawasaki. Bill even touched down the undercarriage of the bike on some of the tighter corners, but we were having too much fun to care. He was a good rider, so I had complete confidence in him. We all had a great time and arrived home safely, with a grin, ear to ear.

My ride to work included crossing the Westgate Bridge. Nowadays, congestion nearly brings vehicular traffic to a complete halt, but in the mid to late eighties, I was able to keep to the speed limit which was then 100 km/h right across the bridge. Nevertheless, when a strong northerly or a south-westerly wind was blowing, the limit was reduced to 80 km/h. But I remember having to fight against the cross winds, leaning the bike into the wind, trying to keep from being pushed into the next lane.

On another occasion, a south-westerly change hit just as I was leaving work. Not only was there a strong headwind, but there was a heavy dump of slushy hail and rain. The roads in Melbourne are a challenge at the best of times, especially when the ubiquitous tram tracks are wet. But when you add an inch or two of slush to plough through, it increased the difficulty by a factor of ten. Still, I would much rather have been on two wheels than four, and oh so much better than being on the train.

I still have all my riding gear, but it has been a while since I have been riding, either on the front or the back. I am keen to go anytime you feel like riding, although I have gone a bit soft of late. I am now very much a fair-weather rider. Unless, of course, Bill drops by.

The Blade

Almost for as long as he could recall David had a fascination for knives, especially sharp ones, the sharper the better. He remembered being captivated, watching his Grandpa hone the edge of his cut-throat razor on a leather strop before using the razor to shave his beard. He could not understand why his own father used a disposable razor rather than a cut-throat, especially when it seemed to him that his father had just as many cuts and nicks shaving as his grandfather.

David had just turned eight years old when he received his first knife – a pocketknife – when he joined the Cub-Scouts. It was a birthday present from his Grandpa. His mother was none too pleased. As far as she was concerned, knives were best left in the kitchen or on the dining-room table. Only thieves and muggers carried knives in their pockets. But on this occasion, she lost the argument. Nevertheless, she made it clear that the knife was only to be used on Cub-Scout activities.

David wore his Cub-Scout uniform with pride, his knife safely tucked in his trouser pocket, attached to the end of a lanyard that he wore over his left shoulder. His Grandpa showed him how to care for the knife and to keep the main blade sharp and the hinges lubricated. Using an old oil-stone that he had in his shed, he showed his grandson how to whet the blade. Holding the blade parallel to the oiled stone, the sharp edge away from him, and with his left pointing finger pressing firmly on the tip, he would make a circular anti-clockwise motion with his right hand firmly gripping the handle.

Besides honing the edge of the pocket-knife, his grandfather showed him how to care for different types of knives. Grandpa had a stash of knives that he kept hidden in his shed. There were several hunting knives, a fishing knife, a boning knife, a set of throwing knives, two stiletto knives, a switchblade and, his prized possession, a Bowie knife with a buffalo horn handle. All of the blades were kept razor sharp.

David was also shown the various uses for the different knives. Some knives were best used for stabbing, others for cutting, others still for slicing. His Grandpa also showed him how to throw a knife at a target, not just the dedicated throwing knives, but also the Bowie, hunting and stiletto knives.

In his junior years, David was careful to obey the directions of his mother with respect to the use of his pocket-knife. But as he grew older, he became less scrupulous and much more secretive. After his grandfather died, he had no one to hang out with and nowhere to whet the blades of his knives. I say blades and knives, rather than blade and knife, because David's collection grew with each birthday, courtesy of his Grandpa, not that his parents knew. It would remain a secret between the two.

But when news came that his grandfather had passed away, David went straight to his room, ostensibly to mourn his loss, but in reality, to work out how to make sure that no one else would get their hands-on Grandpa's secret stash of knives.

David kept his own stash in an old metal trunk that was his father's when he served in the Air Force before David was born. The trunk had been discarded with lots of other junk in the garden shed at the back of the yard. He had acquired a padlock from his grandfather, and kept the key in a special hiding place in his bedroom. The trunk itself was covered with piles of boxes filled with ancient magazines from David's father's youth. It was the perfect hiding place, just as long as no one decided to clean out the shed.

David's grandfather did not need to keep his stash of knives under lock and key, but they were stored in a secret place in his workshop at the back of his garage. Other than his grandfather, David was the only person who knew where they were hidden. And now that his Grandpa was gone, he had to make sure they remained a secret.

After an early night, David woke at 4:00 am, got dressed in his navy-blue tracksuit and, as quietly as he could, opened his bedroom window. The night was cold. The full moon was low in the sky, but there was enough light for him to see. Even so, David could probably have found his way blindfolded. But it certainly helped that his grandparent's house was across the street from his.

He was startled by a dog barking at the end of his street. Just then a Police car drove slowly past, a spotlight shining at the houses and vacant yards as they drove past. David ducked behind a bushy tree until the car was out of sight. He made his way to the workshop and felt around inside for an empty oil drum under the workbench. He removed the lid and reached inside for the oiled leather roll that protected Grandpa's stash of knives. He would have liked to have had the use of a torchlight, but with the Police patrolling nearby, that would not have been a wise choice.

By 5:00 am, he was back in his bedroom. He changed out of his tracksuit and went to bed to wait for the dawn. David did not have time to hide his grandfather's stash of knives with his own, so he hid them in his bedroom on top of his wardrobe under some spare bedding. He just hoped that no one went in search of bedding while he was at school.

David missed his grandfather terribly. With his own father often away from home on business trips, or working late in his office in town, David spent much of his free time with his

Grandpa. But now that he was gone, David sorely missed his company, his advice and his mentorship. It was no exaggeration to suggest that his grandfather played the role of his surrogate father.

A new boy, Bryan Davis, started school mid-term after his parents moved into the town. Bryan was tall, good looking, smart and a sportsman. He was also a bully. David was also smart, but he was of average height and of ordinary appearance. What is more, he preferred the School Library to the Football Field or Basketball Court. He soon came to the attention of the bully.

David had few friends at school, and when Bryan made it known that he disliked David, those who were once numbered as his friends, vanished. David was teased, pushed, punched and, at times, kicked. None of the other boys in his year was brave enough to stick up for him for fear that they too would become victims of the bully. The teachers did not seem to notice, or if they did, to care, and his parents always seemed to be too busy to listen. Where once David would have taken his concerns to his grandfather, he now felt abandoned and alone.

Never one to turn to violence, David eventually came to the realisation that the only way to stop the bullying was to stop the bully. He could not rely on his parents, his teachers or his former friends, so he knew that he would have to stop Bryan himself. But how? Slowly, a plan of action began to form in his mind.

The first item on David's schedule was to find out where Bryan lived. The bully drove his own car to school, where David caught the bus. All he had to do was to see in which direction his nemesis drove and then take the appropriate bus. It took several attempts before David caught the right bus. It turned out that Bryan lived on the other side of the main road that bisected the town, all up about ten blocks away from where David resided, as the crow flies.

David's mother played Bridge every Friday night, while his father would be working late this Friday. After work, his father usually went to the Club, so this Friday seemed to be the right time to put his plan into action. In the days leading up to the night in question, David packed several of his knives into his rucksack, as well as a balaclava, a black polyester jacket, two pairs of gloves (a woollen pair and a rubber pair), a newspaper and a cigarette lighter.

Just after 8:00 pm, David left his house. He kept away from streetlights and hid when a vehicle passed by. He took an indirect route, so it took nearly two hours to reach Bryan's street, but when he arrived at his house his heart sank when he saw that the bully's car was not in his driveway. He felt dejected and was just about to leave when a car turned the corner at the end of the street. David hid behind a bush as Bryan's car turned into his driveway. With his heart thumping in his chest, David felt for the stiletto knife. But Bryan was already out of the car and inside the front door before he could move.

David crept as quietly as he could from his hiding place, down the side of the house, stopping at the back corner. He could see lights go on in the bathroom and hear the toilet flush and the bathroom sink tap. When the bathroom light went out, another light went on which David assumed to be Bryan's bedroom. He crept closer and peered through the mesh curtains; it was him. The bedside light came on and the main light was extinguished, then the bedside light was turned off and all was dark. About 15 minutes later, the gentle sounds of sleeping could be heard from the half-opened window. It was time to act.

David left the bedroom as quietly as he had entered it. His

heart was still beating as furiously as it had when he had thrust the blade into his victim's heart. For his part, Bryan did not know what had hit him. One moment he was lying on his back asleep, snoring, the next he was dead; the stiletto had done its job.

Both the house and the street were quiet as David made his escape. He wanted to run, but a running figure always attracts attention, day or night. There were barely any vehicles on the road, just the occasional Taxi or Uber, and the odd Police patrol. Still, he was careful to avoid lighted areas. The only people he met were either drunk or homeless. He kept his hand on his switchblade in his pocket in case he ran into a mugger.

In a quiet park a couple of kilometres from his house, he found a garbage bin with a lid on a chain. He wrapped his gloves, balaclava, poly jacket and stiletto blade into the newspaper and set it alight, threw it into the bin and closed the lid. He then ran as fast as he could to an area that gave him cover, but from which he could observe movements in the park and the surrounding streets. He waited until he was sure that the fire had not come to the attention of the Police or Fire Department.

Then he walked home.

The murder of Bryan Davis was all the talk at school the following Monday morning. David, as well as all his classmates were offered counselling. Some of Bryan's closest friends were also questioned by the Police Detectives from the Homicide Squad. No one thought to mention that David had been a victim of Bryan's bullying, because no one thought that David was capable of murder.

The Police never solved the crime.

Riding Alone

Riding a motorcycle is one of life's more pleasurable pastimes. In fact, I do not think there is anything more enjoyable than riding a motorcycle on a warm, calm, sunny day. And of course, something this enjoyable is best shared. Besides the practical issues of breakdowns and safety – should something happen to one, the other can offer assistance – there are the joys of a shared experience that can be talked about, argued, discussed and bragged about for days, weeks and even years to come. The trouble is, trying to get someone else to ride with, whether riding another bike or as a pillion with me on my bike, more often than not, is an impossibility.

A case in point. I called a mate last week, 'The forecast's lookin' good for Sunday; d'ya wanna go for a ride?'

'Love to mate, but I gotta take the kids shoppin'.'

There are a million and one things that crowd into our lives and consume our time, that take us away from being able to enjoy some of life's more pleasurable pastimes. Not that I am about to get up on my high horse about others. I received an e-mail from another mate with whom I had been corresponding with for a while. He invited me for a ride last Saturday. My excuse for not going: domestics!

So, what to do? Sunday arrived; a lovely day and the bike was already washed and fuelled and, because it is a classic, albeit a modern classic, all the fasteners were tightened, cables lubricated, and the chain adjusted and oiled. I had no other plans for the afternoon so I am raring to go. I ask the missus and my son in turn if they would like to come for a ride with me. Neither of them showed any interest. So, not wanting to waste the afternoon watching some inane show on the television or worse, I leathered up, donned my helmet and I was out the door and gone – alone.

I took off at a fairly leisurely pace toward Maitland via the back road, sticking pretty much to the speed limit. Just as I passed the turnoff to Morpeth, I made a mental note as I spied two police cars stopped by the side of the road. About 10 minutes later, one of those cars was behind me, lights flashing and sirens wailing. I pulled to the edge of the road, but the highway patrol car raced past me and without stopping. Phew, he obviously had bigger problems to deal with than me. Five minutes later again and I was surrounded by more police cars in two lanes waiting for the traffic lights to change – one beside me and the other behind. I took off at a gentle pace with the rest of the traffic onto the New England Highway; I was on my best behaviour. Pretty soon and they too had gone and I could relax and start enjoying myself.

I eventually turned off the highway and onto more sparsely populated roads. However, I still kept more or less to the speed limits, just enjoying the day, the ride and the roads. Broke Road, from Singleton to Broke, was made to cater for tourists visiting the many dispersed wineries; but it may as well have been purpose built for motorcyclists. Not being as well known as nearby Pokolbin, there was not as much traffic to worry about. The surface of the road is smooth and wide, the corners open and flowing. When other vehicles are encountered, they are easily despatched. I increased my pace a tad revelling in the occasion. Can life get any better?

I missed the turn off to Milbrodale and so I had to turn around. The bike is big and ponderous and not very manoeuvrable at pedestrian speeds. I make a mental note to get in some more practice in the local shopping centre car park. But eventually I was heading down Milbrodale Road. After crossing the narrow, single lane bridge, I found myself on an almost equally narrow road, barely two cars wide. The road was well surfaced with plenty of open corners, but the traffic coming towards me gave me a few scares as some drivers decided to take a generous helping of my side of the road. After a few kilometres, I once again turned around and headed back to Broke. I had seen enough of the road to suggest that it required further investigation, but not today.

Back on Broke Road, I continued on to Wollombi. The road narrowed significantly after Broke and, with three further single-lane bridges, a great deal of care needed to be taken. Fortunately, there was little traffic and what there was was easily dispatched. I rode into the small village of Wollombi, famous for its tavern and noticed the large number and variety of motorbikes lined up out front. Another u-turn, this time in front of an audience and I happily park my machine line abreast with the others, without too much embarrassment. Bikes came and went in groups of two and three as I sat on the verandah and sipped from my stubbie of ginger beer. I was not with anyone, and no one approached me or made me feel welcome to sit and join them at their table. That is how it is at times. I nodded to a few other riders, but they all had partners or mates to talk to and drink with and, presumably, ride with.

Having satisfied my thirst and made the necessary pit stop, I re-donned my gear ready for the ride home. Wollombi Road to Cessnock was nothing to write home about. It was (and probably still is) very bumpy, as if the roller that made it was egg-shaped. It may have been that the road was constructed over one of the many coal mines that dot the area. The old diggings may had collapsed and the earth above had subsided. But more likely, it was just another example of a poor, neglected, secondary NSW road.

I arrived home about half four with a grin from ear to ear, just bursting to tell someone about the ride, especially as my motorbike had performed faultlessly. I love riding, and I love sharing my riding experiences, which is one of the reasons I write. However, I would prefer to be able to share my actual experiences with someone else one on one, rather than having to write about them in such a fashion that others can understand. They say that a picture is worth a thousand words. A shared experience is easily worth that.

 I will continue to ride on my own while ever I have my bike and my health, the days are warm, calm and sunny and no one else wants to come with me. One of these days, when I call my mate, he is going to say 'Yeah, let's go.' But, until that happens, I will just be riding alone.

Going Two-Up

With ANZAC Day fast approaching, any mention of Two-Up conjures up thoughts of groups of people, full of booze and bad manners, standing around in a circle, while someone at the centre tosses up a pair of coins, usually old pennies hoping for a pair of heads when they land. There are shouts of glee when the coins fall in favour of those who have placed their bets and won, while those who have lost swear and scowl at having to pay up.

But not being a gambler, at least not in the accepted sense of the word, I have never played two-up with coins. Going Two-Up for me, and for those who ride, is to carry a pillion on the back of a motorcycle. Ever since I got back into bikes a couple of years ago, I have tried in vain to get my other half on the back of the bike with me. I have taken my son a couple of times, although he now thinks it is too boring and would rather play games on the computer (how boring is that?). I have also taken one of his mates and I have taken a neighbour. However, my wife has so far been very reluctant to get on the back with me to go for a ride.

Now I can understand her reluctance to go for a ride with me on the back of a motorbike. She has vivid memories of seeing me lying up in hospital with one leg in plaster and the other with bits of a meccano set holding it together. I still have those bits set in wood on my desk, but that is another story. Still, I have been out of hospital for well over 20 years now and the wounds have healed pretty much.

But apart from that, I could see no reason why she would not want to come for a ride. So, we sat down and talked about it; turned out that she was scared. Anyway, to cut a long story short, the other weekend, she finally acquiesced and decided to climb on the back for a short ride to visit some friends. Not having been on the back of a bike for a long while, she was not quite sure of what to do, especially coming into corners. We had a few "moments" going through one particular roundabout but otherwise we got there and back without too many problems.

Last weekend, I wanted to go for a ride – the weather was absolutely perfect and it was too good to waste sitting at home. With double demerits for speeding, it was not going to be a "mach run", so when the missus said that she would like to come too, I was delighted. This time I gave her a bit more instruction about what to do when we came to a corner – to lean with me, not more, not less. She listened well and the ride was delightful, apart from a jerk in a 4WD who was busting a gut to get past me through a small town and double unbroken lines.

I took the back road out through East Seaham and on through Clarence Town to Dungog. The road was fairly quiet, apart from the jerk, and the ride was very enjoyable. The air was warm, and it felt more like late summer than mid autumn. When we got to Dungog, we stopped at a café for a coffee and a snack. Rather than returning back the way we came, I took one of my favourite roads, the road from Dungog to Stroud, which is fairly windy and usually without too much traffic. The road has improved recently, with resurfacing work having been undertaken over the past six months. However, this road improvement meant that the road is more enticing for other road users and so we had to share the road more than usual. Still, we had a good time.

We turned right on to the Bucketts Way where the traffic volume increased, and soon enough we were on to the Pacific Highway where the traffic was even heavier. Everyone seemed to be in a great rush to get home (or somewhere) but the stream of brake lights on the cars ahead warned of a problem. Sure enough, one of the state's finest was off on the shoulder with his radar gun aimed in my direction. But not this time, Mr Plod. To get away from the traffic and the state revenue raisers, I made a b-line for Italia Road, which was blissfully quiet. The run home from there was magic.

All in all, a great ride on a great day. As for the missus, she may not be the pillion in a million, but a two-up ride, is better than going-alone, any day.

Once Bitten …

1988 was a memorable year for Australia. It was the year that we celebrated the Bicentenary of European settlement. On the 26th January 1788, Captain Arthur Phillip landed at Sydney Cove in Port Jackson, to begin the first permanent white settlement (or invasion, depending on your point of view) of the great South Land, Terra Australis. The celebrations in Sydney on 26th January 1988 drew hundreds of thousands to watch the tall ships lead an armada of ships and boats down Sydney Harbour, past the now famous Opera House and Harbour Bridge, to commemorate the arrival of that first fleet, 200 years before.

I know this, not because I watched it live, but rather I saw photos and news clips of the event months later. You see, 1988 was memorable for me for other reasons. On 26th January 1988, I was doped up to the eye-balls on morphine after coming to grief on my motorcycle. Exactly two weeks earlier, I was returning home from work, when I turned left in front of a car that I thought was also turning left. He clipped the back of my bike and I went over the high-side, smashing my right leg on the gutter and snapping the ligaments in my left ankle. I subsequently spent the next 11 weeks in hospital, endured numerous operations and have some very vivid scars to show, not to mention memories to share.

But 1988 was even more memorable for me, because it was the year that I stopped riding a motorcycle. The collision with the car changed my life, as well as the course of my life. It changed my life, not only for the physical damage it did to my legs, but the mental damage it did in depriving me of one of the most pleasurable activities that I had ever been involved in

– riding a motorcycle. And it changed the course of my life because for a number of years, my only form of transport would be by motor car.

I got my first motorcycle when I finished high school, as a cheap form of transport for commuting. My good mate was in to bikes in a big way and ported the barrel of my 80cc Suzuki two-stroke and fabricated an expansion chamber (without baffles, mind you). It went like stink, but handled horribly, as you would expect.

Then, after I joined the Air Force and started to earn a decent income, got married and bought a reasonably good car and a house, I gave bikes away completely, well, for a time. I never did get my motorcycle licence on the little two-smoke, so in the early '80s I bought a Suzuki 250, rode it around the block for the local copper and got my licence. But I came to grief a couple of times and gave riding away again.

Several years later and I found myself as a commissioned officer and posted to Victoria Barracks on St Kilda Road in Melbourne. Parking was impossible and commuting by train was a long and tiring activity, so I got my first "big" motorcycle, a Suzuki 750, to commute to work; I lived on the western outskirts of Melbourne at the time. I rode all year round, even through bitterly cold, wet and miserable winters. I loved riding: I loved going to work, because it meant that I could ride; and I loved going home, because I could ride. I rode through the week, and I rode on weekends; I rode on my own, and I rode with friends; I rode down the Great Ocean Road, on the back roads around Ballarat and the You Yangs, up through Lilydale and the Black Spur, everywhere. Melbourne may not have great weather, but it sure has some great roads for riding bikes. Then, everything changed on 12th January 1988.

So where is all this leading, you might ask? Well, once

bitten with the motorcycling bug, you never completely recover. It took me more than 15 years, but I bought myself another motorcycle. My life had been consumed by work, caring for my wife who had a serious illness and caring for our young son. I had no "me time" and my health was suffering as a result. I needed something as an outlet for the stresses and frustrations that were building up in my life. I argued that, being a little older, I might also be a little wiser, and wouldn't put myself in another situation like I found myself in 1988. And besides, I wouldn't be regularly commuting this time, except when the weather is exceptional.

That is not to say that I did not feel vulnerable – motorcycling **is** a dangerous activity because riders **are** so vulnerable. We need to look out for ourselves, and for one another. But I weighed up the potential costs and dangers against the expected enjoyment, and found that it favoured a return to riding, again. I joined the Ulysses Club, and anticipated many years ahead of enjoyable riding and camaraderie with other members of the club.

Sadly, things did not work out that way. While I had a few rides with the Ulysses Club, I had not anticipated that it was more of a social club for senior motorcyclists, rather than a motorcycle club for seniors. Well at least the local version was anyway, so most of my riding was either alone or with a mate.

Then, over time, my health, and in particular, my balance really started to impact my riding. I had had a series of bikes over the intervening decade, which ended with my beloved Muell, a Buell Ulysses. My balance issues were really accentuated on this motorcycle because of its long-travel suspension. I fell off it a number of times while at a standstill, much to my frustration and embarrassment, until I realised that it was time to give up riding motorcycles completely.

But that is not to say that I am giving up riding. While my

saviour is not a motorcycle as such, it is the next best thing: a three-wheeled Can-Am Spyder Roadster RSS SE5 in Dragon Red. I really do not know how much longer I will be riding – that is in the hands of the Lord – but you can be sure of one thing, I will be doing so for as long as I physically can. Because, once bitten ...

By a Hair's Breadth

I normally drive to Stroud for the Writers Group meetings, but the forecast was for a fine, warm and sunny day – perfect weather for Spyder Ryding. As predicted, the morning dawned fine and sunny, and getting warmer by the hour. I was up early – 6.00 am – so that I could get all of my chores done before I was due to leave at 8.10 am. The ride to Stroud is an easy 40 minutes, but I usually leave about 10 minutes early to make sure that I am on time (that is what 30 years working for Defence does to you).

The road between my home and the Bucketts Way, the turnoff at Twelve Mile Creek that leads to Stroud, Gloucester and the Thunderbolts Way, is dual-lane freeway; the only danger is the rising sun in the eyes and police radar traps. But at this hour, with daylight savings still a few days away, the sun was already high enough not to be a distraction, while sticking to the speed limit meant that 'the boys in blue' were no threat to me. I made it to the Bucketts Way turnoff in good time.

The Bucketts Way starts off well sealed, but in a very short distance, the patched potholes make their presence felt. It takes a lot of concentration to keep the Spyder from bouncing off the road. And the further you ride, the more difficult it becomes. Still, if you were put off by rough roads then, sadly, you just would not ride at all in NSW. Our B and C roads must be the worst in the country. I have only ever ridden in NSW and Victoria, and so I can only compare our roads with those south of the border; to put it bluntly, ours are a disgrace. But I digress.

In spite of the road, I was enjoying the ride – how could you not! But, a few kilometres after Limeburners Creek Road turnoff and a few kilometres before the Allworth turnoff, I came around a corner and saw a semi-trailer coming toward me. He was on his side of the road, and I was on mine. However, overtaking the semi was an idiot in a dark blue/green Commodore on my side of the road. He had already used up the separation line allowing for safe overtaking, and now he was overtaking over a solid separation line and heading straight for me. I did not have a lot of time to react because the idiot just appeared from behind the semi.

My first reaction was to stomp on the brakes. I am glad that I did not try the non-existent hand controls because, as you may know, the Spyder does not have them. As I was braking, I steered toward the edge of the road. In fact, with so little room, I actually had to steer such that my left tyre went off the road and into the gravel by the roadside. Things happened so quickly that I did not have time to come off the power. So here I was, the Spyder was half off the road bouncing (bouncing is such a gentle word, it was actually bucking like an out-of-control Brahman bull) over the bumps and holes as the car and semi-trailer went sailing past.

How I missed the car, only God knows. We must have passed each other by a hair's breadth. As I regained control of the Spyder, I came off the brakes and eased it back onto the road. My heart was racing at a million miles an hour. As you could imagine, I slowed down somewhat.

If I had been in a car, there was no way I could have missed the idiot or missed the trees that lined the road. But at least I would have had all the metal of the car and airbags to protect me. If I had been on a motorcycle, I may have squeezed past the car, but more likely, I would have laid it down in the gravel on the side of the road, and maybe even slid it into a tree.

Thank God I was riding the Spyder with its ABS brakes and

stability control. Without them, I would have been in a lot of trouble and, probably, a lot of pain as well.

The Adjutant

He had been in the Air Force for a bit over 14 years, enlisting just before his nineteenth birthday. Over that time, he had been posted to units as far afield as Richmond in NSW, Butterworth in Malaysia, Fairbairn in the ACT, and Point Cook and Tottenham in Victoria. He had even had a stint at Victoria Barracks in Melbourne after he had been commissioned from the ranks. Yet, in all of that time, he had never been posted to an operational squadron. The closest he had been was when he was posted, for a little over twelve months, to Number 486 Squadron, which was the maintenance unit for the Lockheed C130 Hercules transport aircraft flown by Numbers 36 and 37 Squadrons.

Since the time that he had enlisted, he had certainly taken every opportunity that presented itself to him to go flying and, while he did not have a logbook, or receive flying pay, he could boast of flying in no less than twelve different aircraft types in those 14 years. He had even taken over the controls and actually flown a number of aircraft himself, although there had always been an experienced pilot either in the left seat or the front seat.

So, you can imagine his excitement when he was told of his positing as the first Administrative Officer to the recently reformed Number 76 Squadron located at RAAF Base Williamtown NSW, the premier fighter base in Australia. 76 Squadron had a long and illustrious history as a fighter squadron, having been formed in 1942 during the dark days of World War 2. Armed with Kittyhawk fighters it was to be stationed at Milne Bay under the command of legendary fighter pilot CO, Squadron Leader Keith 'Bluey' Truscott. Since that time, it had been equipped with a number of famous aircraft including the Mustang, the Sabre and the Mirage, to name but a few. Since it had reformed, it was no longer an operational unit per se, in that it did not fly operations against an enemy, but it did train pilots to fly operations, so it was the next best thing. And besides, the squadron had aircraft; in fact, it had two types, both trainers, the Macchi and the Winjeel.

The Macchi, affectionately known as the fanta-can because of its orange colour scheme, or the Hoover, because it had more suck than blow according to its pilots, was the aircraft used to teach newly qualified pilots the intricacies of flying a fighter aircraft, and it was used to weed out those unsuitable for flying fast jets. Those who made the grade went on to fly the F/A-18 Hornet or "Pigs" (F-111), while those who did not make the grade were sent to fly "trash-haulers" (Hercules) or P3 maritime surveillance aircraft. The Macchi was also used in flying fleet support training operations against Navy vessels, usually either destroyers, frigates or patrol boats.

The Winjeel, on the other hand was used as a Forward Air Control platform for Army operations calling in close air support (CAIRS), usually Hornet ground attack or F-111 bomber aircraft. The Winjeel first saw service in 1955, so it was one of the oldest aircraft in the inventory of the RAAF. It was not affectionately known as anything (not many had any affection at all for the old machine), although its operators called it the bug-smasher.

The new Administrative Officer arrived, bright-eyed and bushy-tailed at 0730 hours, just to make sure he wasn't late. At 0800 hours, all of the officers went to morning brief, and he was introduced to all of his new colleagues as the new Adj (short for Adjutant), and for the next 20 months, that was how he was referred to, especially by the officers in the squadron.

With the briefing over and done with, the Adjutant

followed the Commanding Officer (CO) to his office for a more personal briefing. It was in the CO's office that the new Adjutant had learnt that not everyone was happy with his arrival at the unit. Thankfully, that did not include the CO himself, who was more than satisfied with the new boy. No, the Orderly Room Sergeant and the new Adjutant had a bit of history going back to their recruit training days when they were on the same course. It did not auger well if the Adjutant's right-hand-man was already off side with him. Still, as far as the Adjutant was concerned, the problem was the sergeant's, not his.

The CO went on, 'The role of the Air Force is to fly and fight. The role of those who don't is to support those who do.' With those words, he impressed upon the new Adjutant that he expected him to support the CO and his staff of instructors and engineers in every way possible during his time at the squadron. He also made the Adjutant responsible for all of the students who were posted to the squadron for fighter introductory training. The students were known as 'bograts' and so the Adjutant was OIC Bograts from that time onwards.

One thing the Adjutant soon discovered was that people were rarely referred to by either their name or their rank. Most were referred to by an abbreviation of their title, like Adj for the Adjutant, XO for the Executive Officer/A Flight Commander and SENGO for the Senior Engineering Officer. Others were referred to by their nickname including the CO who was Spike (though not to his face, then it was sir!); the B Flight Commander was Bomber Brown; while the C Flight Commander, was Mook-eye; and so on.

The Adjutant also learnt an old rule about pilots: 'there are old pilots, and there are bold pilots, but there are no old, bold pilots.' Though, if anyone was the exception to prove the rule, it was Bomber Brown, who was fast approaching retirement age during the Adjutant's time at the squadron. As he learned during his time there, Bomber's exploits flying the Mirage fighter during the 1970s and 1980s made him both old and bold.

The Adjutant soon settled into his role within the squadron. Not only was he in charge of the bograts, as an Administrative Officer, he was also responsible for all of the personnel and office administration within the squadron. Administration covered everything from performance reporting, writing reviews, personnel reports and general correspondence for the CO, to maintaining the financial commitments register. Thankfully, the Adjutant was not alone in this task as he had a staff of three clerks in the Orderly Room who maintained the registry and files for the correspondence in, out and within of the squadron, maintained personnel files and leave records, and submitted posting and employment preferences for the pilots, to name but a few. While the sergeant in charge of the Orderly Room had made it clear that he was not pleased to be working for this particular Adjutant, both were professional enough not to let personal animosities interfere with their working relationship.

When the squadron was stood up after it reformed, it had to make do with two old hangars for the maintenance personnel and an old dilapidated set of prefabricated huts for the headquarters. It would be several years before new accommodation was constructed for the squadron. Because of the make-do accommodation, the squadron was made to feel like the poor cousins against the three Hornet squadrons on base, all of which had relatively new accommodation, hangars and protective 'carports' for the aircraft. The Macchis and Winjeels on the other hand were left out in the open, unprotected from the elements. Still, all of the squadron personnel pitched in to make the best of a bad situation.

While training was usually undertaken in and around RAAF Base Williamtown, the squadron often deployed on exercises, flying interdiction sorties against the Hornets, F-111s or naval vessels. Usually, one of the Orderly Room staff members went along to provide administrative support and taking responsibility for paying the bills (accommodation and meals) and ensuring the 'boys' stayed out of trouble. On one such exercise, the Adjutant went along. He soon found out that pilots are happiest when they can enjoy the good life. And so, instead of booking accommodation on base, the person making the bookings, deliberately waited until all of the accommodation on base at RAAF Townsville was booked out, 'forcing' them to stay in a motel in town.

The flight up to Townsville was an experience that the Adjutant would not soon forget; he got to fly in the backseat of a Macchi with the CO up front. They flew from Williamtown to Rockhampton Airport in the first hop, refuelled and then flew on to Townsville. But if the flight up to Townsville was not enough to be imprinted on his memory for life, then the opportunity to fly in the backseat of Bomber Brown for a fleet support mission was the icing on the cake. Bomber Brown was an extraordinarily experienced pilot, having flown fighter jets throughout his time in the Air Force. He was also a pilot of exceptional skill.

Normally, ground support crew do not fly on operational missions, even though it was just an exercise. Still, an exception was made and the Adjutant suited up and attended the pre-sortie briefing: two aircraft would be attacking a patrol boat somewhere off the coast of Cairns.

Having taken off in formation, the two Macchi jet trainers headed out over the nearby reef and towards the rendezvous point, before the planned interdiction with a patrol boat. While the patrol boat captain was aware that his vessel may come under fire from an 'enemy' aircraft, no specific details about this particular operation were provided. And so it was that, having spied the patrol boat some way off in the distance, with Bomber in the lead aircraft, they dived down to what seemed just above wave height and made their approach, flat out, well, at least as flat out as a Hoover can get.

The Adjutant had previously been in aircraft performing aerobatics and enjoyed all aspects of flying, but this experience was the most exciting flying episode of his life. As the small jet made its approach, he was delighted to see that they had taken the patrol boat crew by complete surprise; there was no-one on deck. Having made the pass and recording a direct 'hit', both jets circled around for a second pass. This time, as they flew past, they could see frenzied activity on deck as the crew made their way to the machinegun on the bow. But it was to no avail, as the two small jets escaped before the crew could train their weapons skyward, let alone get off a shot. Speaking with one of the patrol boat crew some time after the action, the Adjutant was advised that they had flown so low that they were below deck height when they popped up and surprised the crew.

That flying was not all about pilots having fun was brought home for the Adjutant after they returned to Williamtown. One of the more experienced squadron pilots, who was flying a Macchi off Stockton Bight, was involved in an incident where a wing separated from the aircraft. As he ejected from the jet which was spiralling out of control, the other wing came around and hit his head as he was ejecting, knocking him out. He landed in the water, but drowned before the rescue helicopter could get to him. As the Adjutant, it was his task to notify the next of kin, as well as the Air Force hierarchy, Chaplains and social workers of the casualty. While this was not his first experience of casualty notification, this was the first time that he had personally known the one who had died. This incident would have a profound effect on him and how he regarded pilots as a whole for the rest of his career.

All good things must end, and the Adjutant was soon due to be posted out. The posting to 76 Squadron had been the best posting of his career to date, but before he was due to depart, the CO arranged for the Adjutant to go flying in a Hornet.

The F/A-18 Hornet was the premier jet aircraft in the Air Force at that time, and to get GF, what is ostensibly a joyride, in a Hornet is a special privilege enjoyed by very few mortals. The Adjutant was introduced to his pilot, a USN exchange officer, and attended the briefing. They taxied to the end of the runway and stopped as the brakes were applied and the throttles were pushed to full thrust. They sat there as the two engines roared away. Then, as the brakes were released and the afterburners lit, the Adjutant felt that he was being pushed into the back of the ejection seat. They quickly gathered speed as they raced down the runway, when all of a sudden, the pilot wrenched back on the stick and they were sent skyward, vertically! It was not until the aircraft reached 20,000 feet that the pilot levelled the aircraft out. They were flying out over Stockton Bight where the weather was clear and there were no other aircraft; they could pretty much do as they pleased. They went supersonic and did some aeros; the pilot even handed the controls over to the Adjutant. As he was to say after the flight, it was the most fun you could have, sitting down with your clothes on.

The Adjutant left 76 Squadron after 20 months a more qualified Administrative Officer, a more accomplished Adjutant, a more experienced officer and a wiser man. His posting to Number 76 Squadron would turn out to be by far, the best posting of his career.

Marching to the Beat of a Different Drummer

> H D Thoreau: If a man loses pace with his companions, perhaps it is because he hears a different drummer.

For as long as I can remember, I have done things differently to other people. I have thought differently, behaved differently, responded differently, worked differently and believed differently. I had not deliberately gone off in my own direction and never made a conscious decision to be a nonconformist – it just happened.

Sometimes there have been benefits in being different to others, but mostly there have just been drawbacks. Try as I might to fit in and to be one of the crowd, I cannot and I do not. As a kid, when you are different and do not fit the norm, at best you were treated as strange, maybe a curiosity; at worst you are bullied and treated cruelly. A kid who is different can have a most miserable existence, and I did. Friends were hard to make and even harder to keep. No one wanted to be friends with a weirdo.

Even as an adult, those around me mostly do not appreciate my quirkiness. This was especially so after I joined an organisation as conformist as the military, which I did. But even those who appreciated my 'differentness' still kept their distance. In a world where everyone wants to be 'in', no one wants to be on the fringe, much less on the outer. Intolerance, discrimination and prejudice become the norm.

So how was I different? Well, I grew up in a family that valued sporting and/or educational prowess. My grandfather had been an Australian champion fighter; my father boxed and played rugby union, while my mother rowed to three Australian championships, and later became a champion bowler. My siblings all competed in the local swimming club, and my younger brother played rugby league for many years. I was the 'four-eyed' skinny weakling with asthma, who hated sport. I tried my hand at a number of sporting activities, but never achieved much success, either because of my size, asthma or eye-sight.

To make matters worse, my average grades in the classroom did not compensate for my poor ability on the field or in the pool. In my high school years, as my peers were growing toward six-feet tall, I was stuck at four feet something; my voice did not even break until I was in my latter years at high school – I was still singing soprano at 16! As a consequence, I was bullied mercilessly by my classmates.

After a failed attempt at teacher training, in an age of rebellion, long hair and the Moratorium against the Vietnam War, I joined the Air Force. I began to drink to excess and started smoking, as much to fit in as anything else. But within a few years I had married and become a Christian, so gave up excessive drinking and smoking.

If you think joining the military is going against the flow, how much more becoming a Christian in the military. When I eventually found a church that I felt comfortable in, it just so happened to be one of the smallest, most obscure, most conservative of churches there is. Furthermore, while most of my peers were happy to drive their cars to work, I started riding a motorcycle. Most people do not realise it, but being in the military is living on the fringe of society. Being a Christian in the military is living on the fringe of the fringe. Riding a motorcycle and being a Christian in the military is even further away from the mainstream. And that is how I felt.

Now retired, I could not just start giving the old bucket-list a big shake, oh no. First my wife got sick and then I became unwell, and my health has continued to decline. But even then, it could not have been a mainstream illness. Oh no, it just so happened to be the most obscure of neurological conditions there is. It took seven years to diagnose. The condition effected my balance, coordination and speech. And so, as a consequence, I started riding, firstly a Can-Am Spyder and then a motorcycle with a sidecar for a while. Now I drive a sports car What is more, I took up writing – I have since written and self-published five novels and a booklet of poetry.

You probably think I should feel special because I am most likely unique in the world. Sure, there are other Christians that I could fellowship with, ex-military personnel that I could meet with, and other writers with whom I could share my writings. But I would like to ride with other Christians and share my writings with others who knew where I was coming from and shared my outlook on life.

I have has always marched to the beat of a different drummer, but it has been a long and lonely road. Maybe, somewhere, sometime I will find someone else to join me on that journey.

136 Hours

The forecast was for an 'east coast low' developing off the Hunter Coast.

We had been through storms before; big, powerful storms, like the one in June 2007 that drove the unladen bulk carrier, Pasha Bulker, onto Nobbys Beach in Newcastle. That was pretty spectacular, but we survived it relatively unscathed. Most of the damage was caused by flooding in suburban areas of Newcastle. There was a lot of rain in that storm, but the winds were not that ferocious. Nothing could have prepared us for the storm that hit the Hunter Coast last week.

The wind picked up Monday afternoon, but I went to bed at the normal time and thought little of how the next week would pan out.

I woke up Tuesday to a blacked-out house. The wind was howling (I was to learn later that the winds were equivalent to a Category 2 Cyclone). The rain was coming in horizontally. On the street outside, garbage bins were being scattered, together with their contents, all up and down the street. I ventured outside to try to right my bin in readiness for collection. I need not have bothered; the garbage truck did not come.

I was soon to discover that, not only was my home blacked out, but the entire town, indeed, much of the entire Local Government Area had been disconnected from the grid. I not only had no power, I had no telephone, so I had no way of calling anyone to report the outage. Indeed, I could not call anyone about anything, and no one could call me.

No power meant: no phone, no refrigerator, no hot water, no stove or oven and no jug. But at least I was better off than those who relied on power to operate pumps. Friends had no water, hot or cold, and no flushing toilet either. But knowing that others were suffering worse circumstances than me did net make it any easier to endure my own hardship.

To make matters worse, I had no way of purchasing what I needed. With the whole town blacked out, there were no restaurants, cafés, shops or service stations. Those who had emergency generators quickly sold out of the essentials: ice, milk and bread. My local hardware store even ran out of LP gas. I could not drive any distance; roads were blocked either by fallen trees or floodwaters.

The food in my freezer quickly thawed out, and the food in my refrigerator began to smell. We cooked what we could, but meat pies and sausage rolls do not cook well on the barbecue. By the end of the week, we were down to cans of soup, spaghetti and baked beans.

I had never experienced a power outage of more than a few hours. I went to bed Tuesday night with the expectation that the power would be back on in the morning. I was to be disappointed. In fact, I was to be disappointed a lot over the next five days.

By the end of the week, life in Raymond Terrace started to get back to normal. Power was gradually being connected as trees were being cleared from power-lines and the lines repaired. By Friday, the town's business centre was back in operation. The supermarkets were doing a roaring trade. I visited my favourite café and had my first decent coffee in a week.

Saturday was Anzac Day. I took a 'pommy bath', shaved in cold water and headed off to the Dawn Service. Later in the day, a friend who had power invited me over for a hot shower which I gratefully accepted. I did not expect the power to come on a public holiday, so I arranged to have another shower and to do a load of washing on the Sunday afternoon.

By this time, I was becoming quite distressed. It seemed to me that the more well-healed areas had priority over those areas that were of a lower socioeconomic status. I am sure that was not the case, but it certainly seemed that way.

Late Sunday afternoon, I hailed an 'Energex' truck that was passing my house. I asked the driver, 'How long?' He said the 'Ausgrid' people were checking the lines before they could connect the power. As he left, I burst into tears.

The power came back on just after 6:00 pm, a whole 136 hours after it went off.

My New Wheels

I have been driving since I got my car licence after I turned 17 years of age, nearly 47 years ago. I learnt to drive in a clapped out 1957 Volkswagen Beetle that had lousy brakes and no synchromesh in first gear. It had also been involved in a couple of bad crashes, including a rollover after it had been stolen.

But the first set of wheels that I could really call my own was a small Suzuki A80 (the 80 refers to its capacity, yes it was only 80cc). I bought it to provide myself with a means of getting to and from work. It was slow but okay for the daily commute. But, for riding with my mates on weekends, it really was a slug – I struggled to keep up. So, to make it go better my mate ported the barrel, cut off the muffler and made an expansion chamber. It did not have any baffles in the exhaust and it screamed (literally) at full speed, which was only 80 km/h flat out.

When I could afford it, I purchased a car; a Chrysler/Mitsubishi Lancer. It was a fun little car, but I really did not look after it very well. It was also the car that brought me to the attention of the NSW Highway Patrol Police. In just two years, I had racked up enough points and paid enough fines that I was given the choice of losing my licence for three months or going back onto a Provisional Licence for a year. Naturally I chose the latter. As providence would have it, this period coincided with my posting overseas with the Air Force. By the time I returned, I was back on a full licence.

I had two cars while living overseas, one of which was a Sunbeam Alpine, a British made convertible. I was going to call it a sports car, but it was not really all that that "sporty". But it was fun to drive, except when it was raining. On my return from overseas, with a new wife in tow, most of our disposable income was spent setting up our house, although I did swap the Lancer for a Ford Escort.

Over the years, I have had a variety of cars and, when finances allowed, a number of motorcycles. My wife was not too keen on me getting another bike after I had a serious accident on one in the late 1980s. But she had been unwell for some time, and I needed an outlet. Eventually she agreed, and from 1999 to 2015, I had six motorcycles: a Yamaha FZ1, a BMW K1200GT, a Harley-Davidson Road King Classic and a Buell Ulysses XB12X, together with a Can-Am Spyder and a BSA Golden Flash/Tillbrook Outfit. The last two I bought as my own health (my balance) began to deteriorate.

After I sold my last motorbike, I was at a loss. While I had recently purchased a new BMW 3-Series – a lovely car that is a delight to drive on the highway – it just does not have that *joie de vivre* (the joy of living) that riding a bike gives. I knew I could not get another motorcycle, so I started looking around at getting another sports car, this time a real one.

The trouble that I had was that a diet of Mercedes and BMWs had given me expensive tastes; I started looking at the Porsche Boxster. But old Boxsters usually have high mileages and are very expensive to repair when they break down. Newer models are just plain expensive. I had a look at a range of British made MGs (As, Bs, Cs and Fs) and Triumphs (TRs, Spitfires and Stags), but they all had high mileage, and many had equally high prices. What to do?

Mazda's MX-5 is the reinterpretation of the great British sports car of the 1950s, 60s and 70s. They did it so well that, since its introduction in 1989, they have sold in excess of a million cars over four models (NA, NB, NC and ND). The latest model (ND) has just had a mid-life refresh, but instead of making the usual cosmetic changes to the body, they undertook open heart surgery. The 2.0 litre motor now makes 135kW and 205 Nm (up from 118 kW and 200 Nm) in a car that weighs just 1087 kg.

I looked around for some used NC models but finding a low mileage example proved difficult. Then, out of the blue, my wife suggested I get a new one. I was gobsmacked. She argued that a new car would have five years warranty and would be in perfect condition. Who was I to argue? What is more, I found one (a top-of-the-range RF GT with black roof and nappa leather interior manufactured late 2018 but still a current model) at a local dealership at a price $9,000 below the new car price. Bargain!

Most of the cars I have owned and (naturally) all of the motorcycles have had manual gearboxes. However, since 2002, all of my cars have been autos. Indeed, in the last 17 years I have only driven cars with manual gearboxes on three separate occasions, with one of those being the test drive of the MX-5. The Mazda has a six-speed manual gearbox, but it shifts sweetly and the clutch is light. I'm sure I'll get used to self-shifting in no time.

So, if you see a small (they really are tiny), white Mazda MX-5 sports car, whose driver has a grin from ear to ear, it might just be me in my new wheels.

Runaway Bay

Part 1

'You wait till your father comes home; I've had it with you two. Go to your room!'

The ominous warning momentarily instilled a degree of fear into the young teenager. Not that it changed his attitude toward his sister, or hers toward him – they would still hate each other – and so any hope that their mother had that they would modify their behaviour was ill founded.

James sat on the end of his bed, tears welling in his eyes. He felt like a prisoner on death row, waiting for the executioner to carry out his sentence. He was not crying because he was scared, even though he was. He was crying partly from the injustice of the inevitable punishment which was always much harsher than it deserved to be. And partly from years of frustration of playing second fiddle to an older sister who excelled at everything compared to him – academically, on the sporting arena and, most tellingly, in the affection of their parents.

He felt that everyone was against him, that everyone picked on him. At home, there was constant conflict with his spoilt older sister. At school, he was the butt of jokes, the short, goggle-eyed, sickly kid who was bullied mercilessly by his peers. And when he complained to his parents, his father would tell him to stop being a sissy and to stand up for himself – if only he could. And if he complained to his teachers, he knew that the bullying would only get worse. He hated school, he hated his teachers and he hated his father.

James heard the car pull up in the driveway. His heart was

pounding as he heard the door open and close and then the muffled voices of his parents. The door to his bedroom opened. His father stormed into his room yelling, grabbed his right arm and proceeded to whip him on the back of his legs with a leather strap, not once, not twice, but about a dozen times. His father then yelled at him again before turning around and leaving the bedroom, slamming the door shut behind him.

In spite of the pain, he did not cry out. He felt that that would only give his sadistic father greater satisfaction. Nevertheless, great sobs wracked his body as he felt the large angry red welts that had appeared on the back of his thighs and calves. He heard his sister crying and his father almost apologising to her for inflicting some pain. He wondered if she received as many stripes on the back of her legs as he had. Somehow, he doubted it. She was, after all, his "little princess."

James' father was a shift worker, and so he was constantly tired. This perpetual fatigue affected his mood; to James, he was always angry, especially toward him. Because his day-shift at the engineering workshop commenced at 7:00 am, he went to bed early that night. By 10:00 pm everyone else had gone to bed. James waited for the house to go quiet before he stole out of his room and out the back door.

James had been a Boy Scout, and he had kept his rucksack and his sleeping bag in his bedroom. Now the rucksack was filled with a couple of changes of clothes, a pullover, raincoat and the sleeping bag. In his pocket were a handkerchief, a Swiss Army pocket knife and his wallet containing some cash, his student concession card and his bank account access card. He did not know what he would do for food, but he did not want to risk waking his parents by going into the kitchen. His aim that evening was to get as far away from home as possible.

The night was chilly; his breath made clouds of steam as he trudged along under the weight of his pack. The small town was quiet, with only the occasional car driving up the main street. He ducked behind a shrub when saw a police car emerge from a side street ahead, his heart pounding when he saw it turn around. Mercifully, it continued on its way.

In the quiet, still air, he heard in the distance the blaring of a train's horn as it approached a rail crossing. Immediately, he made up his mind to head for the station. Hopefully, a late-night train would take him safely away. Where? Anywhere.

James was roused from his sleep by a cleaner doing his rounds in preparation for the train's next journey.

'Get up mate,' said the cleaner, 'this is the end of the line.'

He looked out of the window and saw, beyond his own reflection, a dimly lit platform. The sun had yet to make its appearance, announcing the start of a new day. His watch said it was only 4:50 am.

'Where are we?'

'Central.'

Even for the busiest station in the City Rail network, the platform at Central Station in Sydney was more or less deserted when James made his way to the ticket barrier. He went through the open gate unimpeded and found himself on the main concourse. A few people had lined up at the ticket window, and some others seemed to be waiting for friends or family to arrive. The McDonalds restaurant was open so he could at least have some breakfast, although he would need to be frugal – he did not know how far his money would need to last.

James had an uncle and aunt who lived in Queensland. Although Uncle Charlie was his father's brother, they were in all respects so unalike. Where his father was always angry at and stingy with James, Uncle Charlie was friendly and generous. Where his father was introverted and reserved, Uncle Charlie was outgoing and gregarious. James secretly wondered if in fact Uncle Charlie was really his father. He would love to be able to live with his uncle and aunt, but Queensland was a long way away, and a ticket on the train would take a large proportion of his meagre savings, even with the student concession.

James thought about it over breakfast and formulated a plan to get to Queensland. He purchased a one-way train ticket to Gosford with the idea of hitchhiking the rest of the way. Although he had been warned many times of the dangers associated with getting a lift from a stranger, he was willing to take the risk, if it meant that he could travel for free.

The commuter train from Central Station to Gosford took a little over an hour to arrive. James alighted from the train, his pack in his left hand, and went to the ticket office to ask for directions to the highway north.

'Where are you headed son?' asked the station manager.

'I'm going to Queensland sir,' replied James.

'The Pacific Highway runs parallel with the train track just outside there,' he said, pointing over his shoulder. 'But if you're heading for Queensland, you're better off taking the freeway.'

'How do I get to the freeway then?'

'You turn left on this street here, turn right at the bottom of the hill – that's the Central Coast Highway – and then you follow that 'til you get to the freeway.'

James hefted his pack onto his back and followed the station manager's directions on to the Central Coast Highway. The rush-hour traffic was very heavy at that time, with most vehicles heading south to Sydney. No one seemed in the mood to offer a young teenager a lift, even if they were going in his direction.

Eventually the traffic thinned out. James was just about to give up any hope of getting a lift to the freeway when a flat-bed truck pulled up.

'Where you headed?' asked the middle-aged driver.

'I want to get to the freeway so I can hitchhike to Queensland. Can you take me to the freeway?'

'I can do better than that. I'm delivering these gas bottles to Bulahdelah, so I can take you that far if you like.'

'That'd be great, thanks.'

James had only a vague notion of where Bulahdelah was. One of his former school friends had moved there when his father had been transferred to the primary school there. All he knew was that it was north of Newcastle and on the highway to Queensland, which was probably all he needed to know anyway.

James climbed into the truck and settled down on the seat, his pack between his legs.

'I was beginning to think I'd have to walk to Queensland.'

'How long were you waiting?'

James looked at his watch. 'About 90 minutes or so I think.'

After a few moments, the driver asked, 'So what's your name?'

'James, what's yours?'

'Arthur, but my friends call me Artie. What do your friends call you – Jim?'

'I don't have any friends,' replied James. Then he quickly added, 'But if I did have, they'd call me Sly.'

Arthur glanced at his travelling companion with a puzzled look on his face.

James continued, 'My last name's Foxx.'

Arthur nodded in understanding and lapsed into silence as he manoeuvred the truck through some traffic and onto the freeway. Once he had the truck up to cruising speed he asked, 'So Sly Foxx, what's so important about Queensland?'

'I'm going to visit my uncle and aunt – they live on the Gold Coast somewhere I think.'

'Do they know you're coming?'

'No.'

'Where's home?'

'I don't have a home anymore. I'm going to live with my uncle – hopefully.'

The warmth of the cabin and the lack of sleep the previous night conspired against James staying awake. He slept most of the journey, only waking when the truck pulled off the highway and into a side-street that led to Arthur's destination.

'A fat lot of good you were as a travelling companion,' he said in mock outrage.

'Where are we?' asked James as he yawned and stretched.

'Bulahdelah: the end of the road for me. You should be able to get a lift here without too much trouble. There are plenty of semis headed north; they all have to slow down for the town so it's not too much of an issue for one to pick up a passenger.'

James thanked Arthur and the two shook hands.

'Good luck Sly Foxx.'

'Thanks Artie, bye.'

James took the opportunity to find a public toilet and to get a bite to eat and a drink from the service station. He did not know when he would get another chance for either. While he was inside, he asked for a scrap piece of card and to borrow a felt-tipped pen. With these, he made a sign "TO

QUEENSLAND," that he hoped would aid his cause – it did.

James had been waiting for barely ten minutes before a large 18-wheeler pulled up beside him. When he climbed up into the cabin, he found a youngish woman dressed in a blue singlet, denim shorts, a baseball cap and work-boots at the wheel. On both of her lightly muscled arms were an array of tattoos as befitted your average "truckie."

James had difficulty keeping his eyes off her ample bosom as she swung the rig out onto the highway for the run north.

'Thanks for ah, stopping,' stammered James.

'That's alright honey, I needed the company anyhow. What's your name?'

'James,' he replied shyly.

'Nice to meet you James, my name's Sally.'

James continued to stare at Sally's chest, something that Sally either did not notice, or did not care about. Eventually he forced himself to watch the road ahead. The two talked about a range of subjects: from hobbies to horses, from surfing to school, from the weather to working. Neither spoke of home, or family, or friends, and that suited James.

By the time they arrived at Grafton, Sally turned the rig off the highway and into a "truck stop."

'This is where I need to take a rest, honey. I've been on the road since Sydney and I need a sleep.'

'Where are we?'

'Just out of Grafton, honey. We'll get going again at 4:00 am – I need to be in Brizzie by 8:00.

While Sally jumped into the small sleeping cabin behind the main cab, James curled up across the front seats. He spread the sleeping bag over his body and used his pack as a pillow. He was reasonably comfortable, although he wished he had brought his toothbrush – his teeth felt decidedly furry.

'Where do you want me to drop you off, honey?'

Queensland had seemed such a long way away when he was in Sydney; James had not really thought through where exactly he needed to go.

'My uncle and aunt live on the Gold Coast somewhere,' replied James hopefully.

'The Gold Coast is a big place, honey – over a million people. I tell you what; I'll drop you off at a service station. You should be able to find a telephone and call them.'

Having found a large Shell Service Station, James thanked Sally for the ride.

'That's alright honey, I appreciated the company. You take care now; bye.'

'Bye,' said James as he jumped down from the big rig.

Ten minutes later, at just before 7:00 am, he was at a payphone in the service station, leafing through the Gold Coast telephone book. There was only one Foxx listed, at Runaway Bay. James smiled at the address thinking that it was very appropriate in his circumstances. He rang the number.

'Foxx.'

'Hello, Uncle Charlie, this is James.'

'James? Oh James; how are you?'

'I'm fine thanks Uncle Charlie. Ah, I've run away from home; can you come and pick me up please?'

'James, you're a long way away, and I think your father might have something to say about that.'

'Uncle Charlie, I'm at the Gold Coast.'

James gave his uncle the address of the service station. A half hour later, he was on his way in his uncle's car to Runaway Bay.

* * * * *

Part 2

After his phone call that morning, and while Uncle Charlie was picking up James from the service station, James' aunt, Auntie Dos (short for Dorothy), had called James' mother to let her know that he was safe and well. Once James had been picked up and deposited at their home at Runaway Bay, Uncle Charlie had to go to work.

'We'll talk this evening when I get back from the office.'

Uncle Charlie was an accountant and worked in the Coolangatta branch of the Sunshine State Bank, while Auntie Dos worked part-time in a local solicitor's office, although she was not working that particular day. James spent his first day on the Gold Coast with his aunt. They used the time getting to know each other, and James, his new surrounds better. Although Uncle Charlie and Auntie Dos were older than James's parents, they did not have any children of their own.

The home at Runaway Bay was a large, two-story mansion that backed onto one of the many canals in the area. The bedroom that James would be sleeping in looked out onto an inviting crystal blue salt-water pool surrounded by deck chairs and palm trees. Moored at a pontoon at the bottom of the garden was a 16-metre ocean-going cruiser that Uncle Charlie used on weekends to go fishing or just cruising on the Broadwater. James felt like he was staying at an exclusive tropical resort hotel – his very own little slice of paradise. Could life get any better than this, he wondered. When Uncle Charlie returned home from work, he realised that life could get a whole lot worse.

'I called your father today; he was very angry James, and very upset.'

'Dad's always angry, Uncle Charlie, it's why I ran away.'

'That may be the case, but he's still your father. You know you can't stay here.'

'But …'

'I'm sorry, but I'm not going to be held responsible for breaking up your family. Remember, he is my brother.'

James had harboured the fanciful notion that, in time, he would become his uncle and aunt's adopted son and so be able to live happily ever after with them. The news that this would not be happening was devastating for him. He could feel his eyes start to mist up and soon, large tears began coursing their way down his cheeks.

James excused himself from the dinner table, his meal only half eaten, and ran up to his room. His uncle found him there fifteen minutes later, lying on the bed, his head buried in the pillow sobbing.

'I'm going to have to get you another pillow, that one's all soggy now.'

Uncle Charlie had hoped to lighten the mood with a little humour – it did not work. He sat on the end of the bed as James turned over, sat up and put his glasses back on. His eyes were all red and puffy. Uncle Charlie gave him a clean handkerchief to wipe his eyes and blow his nose.

'You've always been my favourite nephew; if I'd had a son, I would have wanted one just like you. But I don't, and you're not my son.'

'But …'

Uncle Charlie raised his hand to signal that he had not finished. 'Your father and I are different, even though we were raised in the same home with the same parents. We've had different experiences, we have different values, and different expectations. But we're still brothers, and we love each other as brothers. I could never allow something or someone to come between us, even if that someone is you.'

More tears started to fill James' eyes, but he did not say anything; he knew that further argument was futile.

'Your father will be flying up on Saturday morning to pick you up and take you home. At least you can have a few days with us before you have to leave.'

James did not get to sleep until very late that night; his mind occupied with ideas about what he should do. Whenever he thought of home, he vividly remembered the fights with his sister and the subsequent beatings from his father. When he did get to sleep, several times during the night he woke up with a start, only to realise he was having a nightmare. He did not want to go back to more of the same.

When James surfaced and came down the stairs for breakfast, he found, leaning against a box of cereal, a note from his aunt who had left for work. The note gave details of where to find lunch and advised him that she would be home at about 3:30 pm. He had the whole house and most of the day to himself.

Although it was now July and officially winter in Australia, the climate in the south-eastern corner of Queensland was temperate. Some days, like this particular day, were quite warm. James had been loaned an old pair of swimming trunks that belonged to his uncle. While they were a little too big for him, they were still better than nothing, and besides, there was no-one around to laugh at him. The water in the pool was a little chilly at first, but his body quickly got used to the temperature. He found the swim refreshing and invigorating.

James did not speak any more of his desire to stay on the Gold Coast or of the dread he still felt about his father's impending arrival. Instead, he was determined that, for the remaining time spent with his uncle and aunt, he was going to enjoy himself.

'What time is dad arriving tomorrow?'

'I think his flight gets in at midday. He wants me to take you to the airport and then he'll be taking you on the next flight back home.'

James appeared to take the news calmly, but inside his stomach was churning at the thought of going back home with his father and what might happen when they arrived there.

'I've really enjoyed my holiday here with you both,' said James easily. 'One day I hope to come back and spend some more time with you.'

'That would be lovely,' replied his aunt as she cleared away the dinner plates. 'Maybe we can take you to see one of the theme parks with your sister – Water World, Movie World and Sea World are great places to visit.'

After dinner, James watched a bit of television with his uncle and aunt before retiring early, feigning tiredness. Then, just as he had done earlier in the week, he waited until the house was quiet, crept out of his bedroom and down the hall to the stairs. His heart was pounding in his chest. Thankfully, his uncle was a snorer, and so any noise he made was drowned out by the sounds from his uncle and aunt's bedroom.

James eased out of the front door, making sure he turned the locking mechanism before closing the door behind him. The sensor-light came on as he stepped onto the driveway, and for several moments he was bathed in light, visible to any prying eyes. Thankfully, no-one was looking his way at that time of the night. With a sense of regret, he walked down the street, away from his uncle and aunt's home. For the second time in a week, he was running away from home.

James did not really know his way around Runaway Bay, let alone the Gold Coast. But as a Boy Scout, he had been taught to navigate by the stars. All he needed to do was find the Southern Cross. Once found, he would know where south was, and therefore east, north and west – east was the ocean and north was Brisbane. The only question was whether he wanted to get to Brisbane, a place he knew nothing about, except that it was the state capital, or should he remain on the Gold Coast. Even though he knew as little of the Gold Coast as he did of Brisbane, at least he had "family" nearby. So, if nothing else, he felt a degree of security by remaining in the locality where he was.

When James had arrived in the semi-trailer with Sally, and subsequently been driven by his Uncle Charlie, he had taken notice of the road signs. He remembered that the main part of the Gold Coast was to the south of his final destination of Runaway Bay. So, with the distant sound of the ocean on his left, he started walking more or less south. After about 45 minutes of brisk walking, he found himself on the Gold Coast Highway. There was a McDonald's Restaurant at the intersection so he stopped for a drink and a toilet break.

As he sat drinking his soft drink, James began to think about where he should spend the night. He still had his backpack and sleeping bag with him, so warmth was not an issue. The weather was fine, so rain was not an issue either. The thing that was an issue was his own safety. At school he had been taught from an early age about "stranger danger." As he thought about the possible threat posed by strangers, his thoughts strayed to the danger posed by people he knew, people like his father. He shuddered at the thought of what his father would say when he arrived at the Gold Coast Airport tomorrow, only to find him missing, again.

'Mind if I sit down?'

The question came from a middle-aged man dressed in a white shirt. On his shoulders were navy epaulettes with a white capital "S" embroidered on each. The insignia and the man's nametag identified him as a member of the Salvation Army.

'Sure,' said James.

'You're out late tonight, aren't you?'

James shrugged his shoulders but said nothing.

'What's your name?'

'James.'

'Pleased to meet you James; my name's Paul.'

James shook hands with the Salvation Army Officer but said nothing more.

'Where's home?'

'I don't have a home,' he replied, then added, 'not anymore.'

James bottom lip began to quiver and he could feel his eyes starting to mist up. But this time he was determined not to cry. He took out his handkerchief and blew his nose. When he was settled, Paul asked, 'Have you had any dinner?'

James nodded.

'Where are you sleeping tonight?'

James shrugged his shoulders again before adding, 'I've got a sleeping bag ...'

'I can offer you a bed for the night ... and breakfast in the morning, if you're interested.'

James did not have to think twice, 'Okay.'

James followed Paul outside to the car park where a white van was parked. Inside were two other teenagers about the same age as James, as well as an older man. There was a strong smell of alcohol mixed with stale cigarette smoke and body odour in the van as James climbed in and sat in the back on the third row of seats.

'Everybody, this is James,' called out Paul.

The two other teens called out their names in reply. The older man, whom James thought responsible for the smells, just grunted.

Paul drove the van past two more McDonald's Restaurants and picked up another three teenagers. With the van now full, he headed to the homeless men's hostel run by the Salvation Army at Southport. When they arrived, another Salvation Army Officer took charge of the men and led them to their beds in the hostel dormitory. Those in need of a shower were provided with a towel and soap.

James had never been inside a hostel before. Having been brought up in a small country town, the nearest he had come to communal living before now was when he shared a tent with other Scouts on a camping hike last summer. He found the sounds and smells of the others confronting. Eventually however, exhaustion overtook him and he fell into a deep dreamless sleep.

The clanging of the breakfast bell simultaneously announced the start of a new day, that it was time to get up and, of course, that breakfast was soon to be served. All around the dormitory, men were stirring.

'What time is it?' asked the man in the bed next to James.

James reached for his glasses and then looked at his watch – '6:30.'

'Bugger this,' said the man, 'I'm going back to sleep.'

James got out of bed, grabbed his backpack and went down the hall to the bathroom. On a chair was a pile of clean towels and, in a container on the basin, small packets of soap. He found an empty cubicle and took a hot shower. With a shower, a change of underwear and a hearty breakfast, he felt much better. As he was finishing his bacon and eggs, a Salvation Army counsellor sat down at the table opposite James.

'Where are you off to today?' asked the counsellor.

James shrugged his shoulders and added, 'Have a look 'round I suppose.'

'Where's home?'

James gave the same answer he gave Paul the previous evening, 'I don't have one.'

'Everyone's got a home, even if it's not a very safe place to be at times.'

James did not reply, but his bottom lip began to quiver and his eyes started to mist up again. He took out his handkerchief and noisily blew his nose.

The counsellor continued, 'The streets may not be a very safe place to be either. Sometimes the devil you know is better than the devil you don't. It's James, isn't it?'

James nodded.

'Too many runaways – teenagers like yourself – come to this place, looking for a little slice of paradise, only to find themselves in lots of trouble. Paradise can become purgatory in a very short space of time. Think about it as you leave here today.'

* * * * *

Part 3

The warning of the counsellor played on James' mind as he wandered down the road, away from the hostel, his pack on his back. He shivered at the thought of devils and purgatory, although he was not quite sure what purgatory was. But by the way the counsellor spoke it must be the opposite of paradise. Still, it was a beautiful warm sunny day; he was probably just trying to scare me, he thought.

The Salvation Army hostel that James stayed in the previous evening was located in suburbia away from the main tourist strip of Surfers Paradise and the Gold Coast. The van that had driven him to the hostel had taken a circuitous route meaning that he was completely disoriented when he arrived. So, with his mind otherwise engaged as he walked from the hostel, James did not realise in which direction he was going. In fact, he had been heading away from the coast, rather than toward it. It was not until he arrived at a large intersection with no road signs visible that he realised that he was lost.

James' watch told him that it was nearly 10:30 am. When used in conjunction with the sun, it also told him where north was. And so he turned around and started walking east, back the way he came.

By the time James found himself back on the Gold Coast Highway, the main thoroughfare that links all of the major tourist areas, it was well past lunchtime – he was hungry and thirsty. In the distance to the south were the high-rise apartments and hotels that indicated the heart of Surfers Paradise. James followed the highway south, but only for a few hundred metres, because he was now in the heart of the Southport shopping precinct; he hoped that he would be able to find some place to eat cheaply.

James had not spent any money since he had arrived on the Gold Coast, except for the phone call to his uncle on the day he arrived and the drink at the McDonald's Restaurant the previous evening. Nevertheless, with no income, and now having to pay for his own meals, at least those not scrounged from a charity, he would need to be very careful to preserve what little funds he had.

Southport, and indeed, the Gold Coast, is not an inexpensive place to stay. Backpackers, and those travelling on a tight budget, usually steer clear of this tourist strip, preferring to stay on the Sunshine Coast or even further north at "Bundy," "Rockie," or Mackay. Even in the "off" season, prices for food and beverages, let alone accommodation, are out of reach of the poor and marginalised of society, which is why the Salvation Army hostel proved invaluable.

The only lunch options available to James on that Saturday afternoon, were either "junk" food or to go hungry. He chose the latter, preferring to fill his stomach with free water from the tap at a public toilet. The toilet block was next to a skate park and, with water now sloshing around in his stomach, he sat for a while and watched a group of mainly teenage boys riding their skateboards, scooters and BMX bikes around the park. Suddenly, the attention of one of the boys was drawn to James. He stopped and called out to James.

'What are you staring at four-eyes?'

James was not sure if the teenager was speaking to him, so he turned around to see if anyone else was within range. No-one else was.

'I'm talking to you four-eyes; what are you staring at?'

When James realised that he was the boy's target, his stomach dropped and his heart began to race. 'Nothing,' he said defensively.

One of the teenager's friends came to James' defence, 'Leave him alone Chris; he's not doing anything to hurt you.'

But Chris persisted, 'You calling me "nothing" four-eyes?'

By now he had closed the gap between himself and James. He dropped his BMX bike on the ground and leaped over a small fence to stand over the smaller lad. James waited for the beating he was sure the bully was going to give him; but it never came. Instead, he heard the voice of his saviour.

'Are you deaf? He said he was staring at nothing.'

The voice came from a tall, blond-headed man who had been taking his young daughter for a walk in the park and had seen the confrontation.

He continued, 'You should take the advice of your friend, Chris.' He emphasised the bully's name. 'This lad may not have been hurting you, but if you don't back off, I will be.'

The bully looked up in surprise. He was not used to having his authority questioned, at least, not in the surrounds of the skate park. He thought briefly about punching James and then running, but his chances of escaping the grasp of the tall, blond man were not good. Instead he warned James, 'You better not come back here four-eyes, or else.' With that, he returned to his bike and his friends.

'Th ... thanks mister,' James stammered.

'That's alright – I don't like bullies. You should get yourself home before they come back.'

'I don't have a home,' said James.

The man turned toward James, looking intensely at him with his piercing blue eyes. At last he said, 'Well then, you'd better come with me.'

James had some misgivings about going with the stranger, even someone who had just saved him from copping a beating. Still, the alternative of remaining in the park and being bullied again was not something he wished to think about.

'What's your name?'

'James; what's yours?'

'Steve; and this is Millie.'

Millie was only three years old and was happily sitting in her stroller while her father pushed her through the park. James noticed that Millie was disabled.

'She has CP – cerebral palsy – in case you were

wondering.'

James had never met someone with CP before, and did not know how to respond. He did not know if it was a disease or an illness, and he did not know if it was contagious.

After a brief pause he asked, 'What's CP?'

'CP's a disorder affecting a person's ability to move caused by damage to the developing brain either during pregnancy or shortly after birth.' Steve was clearly practised in giving the explanation of his daughter's condition. 'Millie can't walk very well, and she can't speak very clearly either, but in every other way, she is a normal, bright, engaging three-year-old.'

'Oh,' said James, relieved.

James had to walk quickly as he tried to keep pace with the long-legged Steve. As they walked, they talked. Steve learnt where James had come from and the circumstances of his sudden departure nearly a week ago. He also learnt of James' uncle and aunt at Runaway Bay. James learnt that Steve was a full-time, stay-at-home dad, and that he was married to Kirin, a lawyer working in Brisbane.

'How come your wife works and you stay at home?'

James was used to the traditional view of the family where the husband and father goes to work and the wife and mother stays at home to look after the children and the house; that was how his family operated.

'You're so old-fashioned James,' Steve teased. 'When Kirin and I first met, I was working as a chef in a fancy restaurant in Brisbane. But when Millie came along, it was easier for me to give up my career to look after the baby than for Kirin. And besides, she earns way more than I ever could; it really was a no-brainer. I still get to cook, and the hours are a great deal better.'

James wondered how much different life could have been for him if his parents' roles had been reversed; if his mother worked and his father was a stay-at-home dad. One thing was for sure, his father would not have been so tired so often, he may have been more patient with James and listened more carefully to him when problems arose at school, and he may have had time to take James to football matches or to Scout camps.

James was brought back to the present when Steve turned into the driveway of an old "Queenslander." The old weatherboard, high-set house was in the process of being renovated by Steve and Kirin. The exterior badly needed repainting, but inside things were different. There was a new modern kitchen where Steve did his magic. The bathroom was new, all of the floorboards had been polished and all of the rooms had been freshly painted. With high ceilings and louvered windows, the place was light and airy, cool in summer and comfortable in winter.

'Hello, we're home,' Steve called as he opened the front door.

'Hello my sweet,' said Kirin in reply. She kissed Steve and then released Millie from the stroller, hugging and kissing her daughter. 'Who's this?' she asked when she saw James.

'Just a stray I rescued in the park. Kirin, this is James; James, this is Kirin.'

With introductions out of the way and Millie taking her afternoon nap, Steve asked 'Would you like something to eat?'

'Yes please.'

The zeal with which James replied to Steve's question made him realise that he had not had lunch. He quickly made some sandwiches which James hungrily devoured.

As James finished the last of his cordial, Steve asked him, 'So, what are your immediate plans?'

James considered the question for a moment and then shrugged his shoulders. 'I suppose I'll try and get a job somewhere.'

'How old are you James?' asked Kirin.

'15, I'll be 16 in September.'

'No one will employ a junior without a parent or guardian's consent,' declared Kirin.

'You could be my guardian,' said James hopefully.

'I think your parents might have something to say about that.'

'And besides,' Steve added, 'you're still too young to leave school. I think they changed the rules recently didn't they – you have to stay at school until you're 17.'

'I'm still on school holidays; school doesn't go back for another week.'

'Well, that gives us a week to get things in order,' said Kirin in a matter-of-fact manner.

James wasn't sure what Kirin meant by getting things in order, but he was glad that he did not have to face making a decision just yet.

'We'd better get the spare bed ready so you have somewhere to sleep tonight then,' said Steve.

Being a solicitor in a small law firm in Brisbane meant that Kirin had a great deal of experience in Family Law matters. Many children have relational differences with custodial parents, and particularly when their parent gets a new partner. These differences increase as children reach adolescence. While James did not run away from a "broken" home, his circumstances were not otherwise dissimilar.

Kirin's first priority was to contact the Police's Missing Persons' Register to advise that James was no longer missing and that he was safe in her care. Next, she needed to contact James' parents to speak with them. Their response would determine whether she also needed to bring in the NSW

Department of Family and Community Services.

James, for his part, spent the week assisting Steve. He sat with Millie while Steve began the enormous task of sanding the weatherboards in preparation for painting the exterior of the house. At other times, he helped by setting the table for meals and washing up afterwards.

On the Wednesday evening, as they were finishing the evening meal, Kirin said, 'I spoke with your mother this afternoon.'

James spoon stopped mid-air. 'What did she say?'

'That she loved you and wanted you to come home.'

'What did you say?'

'I said that there were some issues that needed to be resolved first: like the relationship with your father, and the bullying at school.'

'What did she say then?'

'She said your father has been sick with worry, so much so that he just spent a few days in hospital with heart stress.'

The news that his father had been in hospital came as a shock to James. His father had always been fit and strong. He was more surprised that his father was worried about him.

Kirin continued. 'She said that your father is a changed man James. She said that things would be better at home and that your father has promised that he would go to see the principal of your school and demand that he take action against the bullies. She said that they were both sorry for the way things had worked out and that you felt as though you had no other option than to run away.'

'I'm sorry for the way things have worked out too,' said James, as his eyes started to mist up.

'Life isn't always easy James,' added Steve. 'We thought we had the perfect life together: living on the Gold Coast, working at our respective careers, in a loving, caring relationship – our lives were gold. And then Millie came along and everything was turned upside down. Don't get me wrong – I wouldn't trade Millie for all the tea in China – but sometimes, the gold gets tarnished, and you need to spend time cleaning it up.'

On the following Saturday, Steve took James to the airport where he boarded a one-way flight back to Sydney. His mother and sister met him at the airport. There were hugs, kisses and tears all around.

James went back to school and completed his studies. Eventually, he went to University where he graduated with a degree in Social Work. In time, he found employment with the Smith Family working with teenagers who had run away from home.

A Matter of Trust

Why would someone who is scared of heights join the Air Force, let alone abseil off a cliff?

I have always had a problem with heights. I remember one Christmas that my dad organised a joy flight in a Cessna at the local aero club for us kids. I was fine when we were taxiing on the ground, but as soon as we were airborne, I refused to look out of the window at the ground below – I was terrified.

In the Scouts, I remember we constructed a tower from which a flying-fox was attached. All my mates happily leapt off the tower and rode the flying-fox hundreds of metres to the ground. I was fine climbing the tower, but once I was sitting in the flying-fox, my courage failed. It was only because I was pushed off the tower that I actually rode the zip line to the ground.

So, if I was scared of heights, you would have to wonder why I would join the Air Force? But at least I had a ground job. Nevertheless, over time I began to enjoy flying and I have even piloted an RAAF trainer when I was at Point Cook. The best experience I have ever had flying was in the back seat of an F/A-18 Hornet at Williamtown; we even did some aerobatics.

But there is one thing that I still find terrifying: sky diving. After all, why would a sane person jump out of a perfectly serviceable aircraft? I have never done it, and never plan to either.

One day, a friend asked me if I had ever abseiled. Of course I had not; I was not that stupid. But he encouraged me to go with him. A friend of his was an accomplished abseil instructor and they had planned a trip to the Watagans, so I went.

Standing at the bottom of a 50-metre cliff face looking up is daunting; it seemed a long way to the top. Peering over the edge from the top of the cliff looking down is even more daunting; it seemed an even longer way to the bottom. While there is only one way up, there are two ways of getting down: the coward's way, or over the edge. But I had not come all that way for nothing.

The instructor was very good and strapped me into the harness and showed me what to do. The rope that I would use to abseil down the cliff was attached to a large boulder that was not going anywhere. With instructions to take it easy and look up rather than down, I stepped over the edge. Once on the ground, I immediately returned to the top of the cliff to do it all over again. Despite my initial fear, I really enjoyed the thrill of abseiling and could not get enough of it.

Looking back on my accomplishments, I came to realise that it was not that I was brave or courageous in flying, aerobatics or abseiling. Rather it was a matter of trust. I trusted the pilots that they knew what they were doing, and I trusted the abseiling instructor to get me safely to the bottom of the cliff.

Dressed for the Occasion

Have you ever been to an important family event, only to find that you dressed casually, when the dress code was Formal?

There was a time when a man would wear a suit to an important event or a significant occasion, often that was to church on Sundays. If he did not own a suit, he would wear his best clothes. Indeed, he and his family would wear their "Sunday Best". One elderly gentleman in my church still wears his suit every Sunday, regardless of how warm it is.

But times change. No longer is the wearing of a suit *de rigueur*, except for very formal occasions. In recent years, there has been a more casual approach to the dress code in society. Quite often suits and ties have been replaced with open neck collars and sports jackets. Sometimes, the jacket has been lost, even for such important events as weddings and funerals. Recently, I even went to a funeral in jeans.

So, when I received a wedding invitation from my niece, I decided early on that I was not going to wear a suit. In fact, as I was not part of the bridal party, I was not even going to wear a jacket.

The wedding would be outdoors, in a park, in a suburb of Melbourne in September. Having previously lived in Melbourne, I was acutely aware of the vagaries of the weather. It could be stinking hot one minute, freezing cold the next, and pouring with rain the next. There was a standing joke in Melbourne: if you did not like the weather, wait five minutes and it would change.

I thought I was going to be very smart and wear slacks, a shirt and a jumper. No tie and no jacket. If it was warm, I could take the jumper off, and if it was cold, I would leave it on. What could be better than that?

The family assembled at the hotel before setting off. Both my son and my brother were appropriately dressed in suits, complete with ties. All of the ladies – my mother, sisters and niece – were dressed to the "nines". Everyone else was all dressed for the occasion. I tried to convince myself that at least I would be comfortable.

The family arrived at the car park, and we wandered down to the area where the ceremony was to take place. As more and more people gathered, I began to feel less and less comfortable, but it had nothing to do with the weather.

Every single male in attendance was dressed in a suit and tie. Whether they were in the bridal party, members of the family, or just friends. The only man not wearing a suit and tie was me. I stood out like the proverbial sore thumb.

Each family has at least one member who is a little strange, a touch odd, or a bit eccentric. Someone who is a bit of an embarrassment, who always dresses inappropriately, who is invited to important events, but who the family secretly hopes will decline the invitation. I am beginning to feel that I am that one in our family.

If ever I am ever invited to another wedding, I am going to make darn sure that I dress for the occasion.

Held Captive

I woke up feeling cold and disoriented. As I lay on the floor, I realised that I was inside some sort of heavy vehicle – a truck or a van – the humming of the diesel engine and the whine from the differential as I was being driven along drowned out most other sounds. There were no windows and I was in complete darkness. I assumed it was still dark outside, although there was no way to be certain. I tried to roll onto my side, but my hands were bound behind my back, and my feet were tied at the ankles, so it took several attempts before I could sit up. My head ached and my mouth was dry, and I was hungry, ravenously so. There was also the strong smell of ether on my shirt-front.

Without the use of my hands, I had nothing to stop me from falling down again when suddenly the vehicle slowed and then stopped, but it was only momentarily, possibly for a stoplight. Occasionally I could hear other vehicles as either they passed us, or we passed them. We slowed once more, and this time I was flung across the floor to the other wall as we made a sharp turn. The road had become quite rough and we bounced along for several minutes before turning another corner and coming to a stop. I heard the clanging of a chain, before we started moving, but at a much slower pace. The vehicle made another turn, but I was ready this time and braced myself. We stopped and afterward I could hear some scraping noises and a couple of voices before we started reversing. When the vehicle came to a stop, I could hear voices again.

I shivered as I sat in the darkness inside the vehicle. I heard some scraping noises before a loud bang as if a large heavy door had closed; then silence. I half expected my captors to open the vehicle and let me out, but I was to be disappointed. I waited, but the only sound I could hear was my own breathing and the beating of my heart.

'Hey!' I called, 'Is anybody there?'

There was no reply, so I lay back down. I was deathly tired, but I was too cold to sleep. My teeth started chattering. If there were any noises from outside, they would almost certainly be drowned out. I must have lain there for what seemed an hour or more, but was likely no more than 15 or 20 minutes. Then, faintly, I heard voices. I clenched my jaw and held my breath as I craned my ear to listen. I sat up. There were two voices, a man's and a woman's, but I could not hear what they were saying.

I called again, 'Hey, I'm in here!'

I was still in pitch darkness but I could hear someone at the rear of the vehicle unbolting the door. My heart was pounding. When the door was swung open, artificial light came flooding in. I was momentarily blinded so I had to blink several times before I could see clearly.

'Come down,' the accented male voice ordered.

With my hands and feet still tied, I crawled on my backside, as I tried to comply with the direction. When I got to the edge, two pairs of strong arms lifted me down.

'What the bloody hell's going on?' I demanded as I faced my captors.

In response, I received a well-aimed punch to the midriff from one of the two men. My legs buckled as the wind was knocked out of me.

'We ask the questions around here,' he replied.

With a nod of the woman's head, I was half carried, half dragged through what appeared to be a warehouse. There were several racks of floor to ceiling shelving, now empty. In a corner was an office with a large glass window in the internal wall, and a smaller one in the door. There were no outside windows. Inside the office were a table and several wooden chairs. I was dumped unceremoniously in one of the chairs. One of the men untied my ankles, but my hands were still tied behind my back.

I hunched over the table as I tried to catch my breath. I heard the door close and a key turn in the lock. When I lifted my head, I was alone. The light inside the office had been extinguished. What light there was came from the warehouse fluorescent lights shining dimly through the dirty window.

I sat in semidarkness. I was still cold, tired and hungry, and my head ached even more. I placed my head on the table and must have slept because when I opened my eyes, the warehouse lights were out and the truck was nowhere to be seen. The first light of dawn was brightening the skylights in the roof.

I stood up and went to the door. Through the window I could see the woman sitting on a chair half asleep. I tried the handle, even though I knew it would be locked. The noise woke the woman and she stood and motioned for me to stand back. When she opened the door, I noticed for the first time that she was armed with a semiautomatic pistol.

'What do you want?' she demanded.

'I need a piss and something to eat and drink.'

In the half light of the morning, I could see that she was in her mid 20s, with dark hair and even darker eyes. She was wearing tight denim jeans and a khaki blouse that looked to be a size too small; the buttons straining to keep her breasts contained. In different circumstances, she might even have been attractive.

At first, she appeared undecided about whether to call one of her companions or to take me herself. Eventually, waving her weapon, she directed me out of the office and toward a door marked "Gents". She pushed the door open and turned on the lights. I followed her into the room which had a row of sinks down one wall and an assortment of broken mirrors above. She directed me to go through the next door where the toilets were. The stench of stale urine assaulted my nostrils.

'I can't do it with my hands tied behind my back,' I called through the closed door.

She pushed the door open with her boot and joined me in front of the urinal. She turned me around and, reaching around me from behind, she undid my fly and pulled out my manhood. When I had relieved myself, I shook as best I could before she tucked it back in and zipped me up again.

When I stepped back, I said, 'Hopefully, next time we're intimate, I can return the favour.'

My attempt at humour was greeted by a whip across the face with the pistol. She roughly turned me back around and, with a shove in the back, I was sent sprawling onto the tiled floor.

'There won't be a next time you sexist pig.'

I could taste blood in my mouth, and I looked down and there were drops of blood on the floor from a cut on my cheek. I made a mental note to keep my smart remarks to myself in future.

As I struggled to get to my feet, one of her companions came barging through the door. When he had taken in the scene, he gave a malevolent smile. 'There, there Gretchen, we don't want to damage the merchandise, do we? Best wait until he's of no further use.'

As I was walked back to the office, I looked around the warehouse. In the far corner I noticed another man who appeared to be sleeping on a camp stretcher. There was an electric heater next to him, a microwave on a bench and a couple of eskies on the ground which, I assumed, contained food. The other younger man must have driven the truck away.

My stomach rumbled. I suddenly remembered how hungry I was. I had been taken on my way home from work. Dinner would have been on the table when I arrived. Whenever I am going to be late, I always call; but not last night. My wife would be beside herself with worry by now.

Before the door was locked again, I enquired, 'How about some food? I haven't had anything to eat or drink since lunchtime yesterday.'

The man who was now guarding the door called to the woman. I do not know what he said, but she went over to the man lying on the stretcher. After she had roused him, he sat up. The two were looking in my direction, before she turned and opened one of the eskies and removed some food. She walked back toward my "prison" carrying a bag of what appeared to be fruit, and a flask. When she arrived at the office, the man unlocked the door and opened it for her.

'Ah, room service! What, no bacon and eggs?'

'Be grateful for what you get, pig.'

I certainly was grateful. After untying my bonds, I wolfed down a banana as soon as I had it peeled, and chomped into an apple, while she poured water from the flask into a mug. As I was eating, the other, older man entered the office and motioned the woman to leave. He sat down opposite me and contented himself to watch as I hungrily devoured my breakfast. When I had finished, he called the younger pair to join him.

'Satisfied?' he asked.

'Only my appetite. Normally I'd say thanks, but under the circumstances ... So, who are you and what am I doing here?'

'Don't you remember?' asked the woman.

'No, not really. The last thing I recall is being run off the road. I was coming 'round a corner and there were two sets of headlights coming towards me. I must have hit my head and blacked out.' I shook my head to clear my mind, but all that did was remind me that I still had a splitting headache. 'Then I woke up in your truck with my hands and feet tied.'

'Well Mr Chandler,' replied the older man, 'it is Mr Chandler, isn't it? Mr Richard Chandler, Chief Operations Manager at ROQ. Let me do the introductions: my name is Drakken, and I'm the leader of this band of crusaders. This is Gretchen and Pitr, and we are New Genesis Warriors,' he declared proudly. 'You are our hostage.'

I had never heard of New Genesis, and I did not know what I was being held hostage for or against. I just assumed they were yet another loonie left wing group that hated everything about a civilised society.

'What am I being held hostage for?'

'Your company is killing our people. We will hold you until they stop.'

'But what if they don't stop?'

'Then we kill you.'

My company was a large multinational with offices in New York, London, Johannesburg and Brisbane. They also had mining operations on four continents, and processing factories in a dozen countries.

'Kidnapping a company executive is a rather drastic step to take. Why don't you just protest like all the other groups?'

'We have been protesting for years, but you don't listen. You pay off the police and the politicians to do your dirty work, but no longer. Now is the time we strike back.' He spoke like a religious zealot.

I did not know what he was talking about. As far as I was aware, our operations, at least the ones managed locally, were all above board. The only protests had come from some of the more radical Green groups who objected to our refining operations in the Fitzroy River area in Central Queensland.

'I don't know what you're talking about. We haven't corrupted the authorities here.'

'Oh, not here Mr Chandler, not here.'

My two younger captors joined in. 'Not here, not here,' they said, nodding in unison, like a pair of nodding dogs.

'And then there're the lives your company has ruined, the raping of the landscape, the toxic waste dumps that you've created, poisoning the environment. Someone has to pay, Mr Chandler, and in this case, it is you.'

'Look, my company operates within the law, and we abide with all of our legal obligations. We've complied with the most stringent EIS imposed on any company in Queensland, and we have an impeccable safety record. There have been no deaths and only two minor injuries all year and ...'

Drakken held up his hands for me to stop. 'Mr Chandler, I'm sure that everything you've said is correct, for your operations here, but what about in Borneo, in New Guinea, and in the Central African Republic?'

'I'm not responsible for those operations.'

'Oh, but Mr Chandler, you are, or at least your company is, and since you represent your company here in Australia, we hold you personally responsible.'

'But that's not fair!'

'No, Mr Chandler, it's not, but neither is your company.'

I soon realised there was no point reasoning with these people. They had their own twisted view of reality, and nothing I could say or do would make them change their minds. My only hope was either escape or rescue.

As if reading my mind he continued. 'And don't think for a moment that the cavalry will be coming to your rescue. The fools will never find us here.'

As I suspected, my wife was worried that I had not called her to say I would be late. When I was not home by 8:00 pm, she called my mobile which was still in its cradle in my truck. At 9:00 pm she called my office only to be informed that I had left over three hours earlier. Taking into account traffic and distance, I should have been home by 7:00. That was when she decided to call the police.

At about midnight, a highway patrol officer found my Ford Ranger dual-cab utility in a ditch on a winding road about 45 kilometres from my home. The airbags had gone off and there was superficial panel damage to the vehicle, but there was no sign of the driver. Assuming that I had started walking, he commenced a cursory search of the road, until he was called to a traffic accident on the other side of town. It was not until the following morning after my wife called the General Manager of ROQ, that a more thorough search was conducted.

At noon, a reporter at *The Daily Mail* in Brisbane received a text message:

Richard Chandler, Chief Operations Manager at Resources of Queensland Pty Ltd, has been taken prisoner by the warriors of New Genesis. He will not be released until our demands are met. Drakken

His initial reaction was to dismiss the message as just another crank, but decided to call his contact in the Police Media Unit before deleting it. He was glad he did, so were the police.

The General Manager of ROQ had friends in high places. After the call he had received from Louise Chandler, he placed a call directly to the Commissioner of the Queensland Police

Service. The Deputy Commissioner for Traffic Operations was the first to be summoned. After the text message was received, the Deputy Commissioners for Intelligence, Counter-Terrorism and Major Events, and State Crime were also brought in.

Detective Chief Superintendent Dennis Moynihan was given carriage of the investigation. He called in a team of top investigators from the various Commands to a meeting.

'Has anyone ever heard of New Genesis?'

'No sir, and there's nothing in our database on them.' Detective Inspector Keith Ryan spoke for everyone in the room.

'What about Drakken? Is it a person's name or an organisation? What is it?'

'Can't help you there either sir. Again, there's nothing in our database.'

'Well, get our Intel people to find out, and check with Interpol. Someone somewhere has to 've heard of 'em. Even if they're just a bunch of cranks, they didn't just grow up in the forest like a bunch of Greenie toadstools. And get forensics to go out to where they found Chandler's vehicle. I wanna know if there're signs of another vehicle.'

'I think the vehicle's already been towed out of the ditch,' added another detective.

'Bloody hell and I suppose the boofheads 've already driven all over any skid marks. Who approved that?'

'The local sergeant I suppose.'

'Bloody hell, another constable promoted beyond his capabilities. Well get forensics to run a fine-tooth comb over Chandler's vehicle as well. The local plods 've probably missed something.'

'They did find a wad of cottonwool soaked in what they believed to be ether. It's possible that those who kidnapped

Chandler used that to drug him.'

'Yes, but how did they get to him in the first place?'

'Run him off the road, I suppose.'

'Well, we need to find if there's any evidence of that. And get out to the offices of ROQ; see if they've received any threats or protests in recent weeks. I also want someone to get a statement from Mrs Chandler.'

'Have they made any demands yet sir?'

'No, not yet. The reporter's phone's been checked. The text was sent from a Phoenix pre-paid mobile. We're waiting to see if this Drakken's gonna continue using this means of communication.'

'Do we know where the text was sent from?'

'No, not yet, but if they send another one, we've got our communications crew ready to triangulate. Any other questions? Thanks gentlemen.'

Everyone in the room stood to leave, before Detective Chief Superintendent Moynihan added, 'Remember, the Commissioner himself is taking personal interest in this case, and no doubt the Premier and the media will be too. So, whatever else you're doing, or planning on doing, shelve it until we break it. Okay?'

'Yes sir!' they replied in unison.

I had never been a prisoner before. In fact, I had never even been inside a prison. The closest I had come was when I drove past the Capricornia Correctional Centre on the Bruce Highway in North Rockhampton on my way back from a meeting in Brisbane last March.

I did not think much of prison life, at least not life in this prison. I had been here for less that 12 hours, and I was already bored out of my brain. My wrists, which had been retied after my first meeting with Drakken, were getting sore and my arms and shoulders were cramping up from being bound in one position. The only exercise I could get was walking around the perimeter walls of my small cell. I must have circumnavigated the desk 250 times by lunch.

My captors came and went at regular intervals of what I guessed to be hourly shifts. Drakken disappeared just before a second younger male rejoined the others after the fourth shift change, at what I judged to be midmorning.

Lunch was a somewhat more substantial meal than breakfast. I received a wrapped ham, cheese and tomato sandwich, two pieces of fruit and a can of soft drink. I was even allowed a toilet break, albeit accompanied, but without my hands being tied. We should thank God for small mercies.

As the new guy was returning me to the office cell, I turned around and faced him. 'Do I have to be tied? I mean, there's no way I can escape from my prison. It's not as if there's a secret trapdoor that I can sneak out of, and besides, you can keep an eye on my through the window.' There was a look of hesitation on his face so I continued, 'Come on, look at my wrists; they're already chafing. They'll be raw and bleeding if you tie me up again.' I could see that I was getting through to him. 'If you have any compassion …'

'Andrez!' At the mention of his name, my young captor jumped.

Gretchen approached us from the shadows. 'Don't listen to this pig. If *he* had any compassion, he wouldn't be working for a company that kills and maims, and rapes the environment.'

'You can say something a hundred times,' I declared defiantly, 'but that doesn't make it true.'

'Shut your mouth pig or I'll shut it for you.'

She raised her pistol and was about to strike me across the face a second time when I heard another voice shout from the other side of the warehouse. 'Gretchen! Enough!'

I turned to see Drakken walking quickly toward us.

Gretchen turned to me and said in a low voice, 'Saved for now pig, but I will have my way when I get you alone.'

'Alone with you, ooh I can't wait.'

Gretchen never did get me alone again. Late that night, just as I was settling down to another night in captivity, pandemonium broke out as the Queensland State Police Special Weapons Operations Team launched their attack. They fired a number of stun grenades into the warehouse, outside of my office cell. Then there was the sound of small arms fire. I lay sprawled on the floor in the office, cowering under the desk.

When the firing stopped, a figure entered the office and turned on the light. I peeked out from the edge of my cover. The officer was dressed in a navy-blue battle uniform, a helmet and ballistic armour, and carrying an automatic weapon. As he took off his night-vision glasses, he turned to me.

'Are you Mr Chandler?'

'Thank God, the cavalry's arrived. Yeah, I'm Chandler. I'm glad you found me.'

I did not see what happened to Drakken, Gretchen Andrez or the other guy, but I assumed that they had each been taken out by the SWOT team. I doubt they knew what hit them, not that I cared much.

If Security's the Answer, What's the Question?

I grew up in a home where "Security" was the answer to life's big question, even if I was quite unsure what the question was. My father grew up in the Great Depression where there was widespread unemployment and poverty. He did not want his children to have to endure the hardships that he had to put up with growing up.

Both my parents worked hard to ensure that we would never have to go without. Still, much of dad's income went into his superannuation and investments so they would have a comfortable retirement.

His four children were shepherded into "Government" jobs when we left school. To his mind, a government job was a job for life, and that equalled security. I joined the Air Force.

I struggled during the first few years adapting to the "Service" lifestyle: yes sir, no sir, three bags full sir. But right from the start, I had a goal in mind: retirement. The superannuation scheme then available allowed personnel to retire on an indexed pension after only 20 years' service. So, at 39 years of age, I could retire on a pension – for life! How good was that?

But retiring at 39 is all well and good, if you have another job to go to. A Service pension is okay, but it is not much to live on. So, I had to find another job, at a time when BHP was just closing down. Defence again came to my rescue and gave me a job as a public servant, doing a similar job to the one I did when I served in the RAAF. And as a public servant, I would have access to another indexed pension.

My future financial security was safe, so it was now time to indulge myself. First came the Mercedes Benz car and the BMW motorcycle; a Harley Davidson came later, together with the BMW car and Mazda Sports Car. You know the saying: he who dies with the most toys wins. I was vying for the title.

As I looked forward to retirement, once and for all, my wife and I started to make plans. Like many others, we wanted to travel and started to fill out our "Bucket List". We had never been right around Australia before, never seen Uluru or visited Kakadu. We had never seen the Great Barrier Reef close up or the Kimberleys. And then there was New Zealand, the States, Canada, and … the list goes on.

And then my health failed, and I was forced into early retirement. All the plans we made hinged on continued good health. I now have difficulty travelling overnight, let alone for weeks on end, and I have problems with my balance. I also have poor coordination, and a tremor in my hands, the left being worse. Even my speech is affected. And it is getting worse.

I have been reflecting on my life goals recently. What good is it if your retirement is secure, you have all the money you will ever likely need, and you have all the toys you want to play with, if you do not have the health to enjoy it all? There is another popular saying: we are so busy making a living, we have no time left to make a life. I would like to change it to: we spend so much time saving for retirement, we end up using the savings to stay healthy.

Security is all well and good, but being financially secure does not necessarily mean that you have a life worth enjoying.

In Love with a Pearl[iv]

The Island of Penang, known as the Pearl of the Orient, is located off the north-west coast of the Malay Peninsula. The capital city, George Town, was founded by Captain Francis Light, the father of Colonel William Light, Adelaide's first Surveyor-General. George Town has many beautiful old colonial buildings, with the core recognised as a UNESCO World Heritage Site in 2008. The population of the island is highly diverse in ethnicity, culture, language and religion, with the population made up of Chinese, Malays, and Indians, as well as a large expatriate community.

I have a special affinity with Penang. In my 23-year career with the Royal Australian Air Force, I spent almost four years over two postings living in Penang. When I arrived in 1977 at Air Base Butterworth, located on the mainland opposite Penang Island, it was one of the largest operational fighter bases in the RAAF. There were two squadrons of Mirages, several Iroquois helicopters, a couple of DC-3 Dakotas, a Canberra bomber, a maintenance squadron, a base squadron, a hospital, an Australian Army Rifle Company and the Headquarters of the Integrated Air Defence System. At that time, the Australian military was still involved in operations against the Communist Insurgency on the border region with Thailand.

I was a fresh-faced, naïve 21-year-old. I had never been overseas before and all of the sights, the sounds and the smells were a great culture shock for me. But I adapted quickly and, within three weeks, I had met the love of my life, a week later I had moved off base and onto the Island, and four weeks later again I asked her to marry me. More than forty years later, and we are still together.

There is an old saying: You cannot put an old head on young shoulders. I wish I had known on my first posting to Butterworth, what I knew second time around. I may not have made all the same mistakes or gotten into as much trouble the first time. But, I suppose, that is what life is all about – getting experiences – just as long as you learn from your mistakes, and the experiences do not kill you.

RMAF Butterworth was a very different place in 1990 when I returned to what I had left a dozen years earlier. Instead of an Australian military population in excess of 4,000, we now numbered just over 400, with the majority made up of the Australian Army Rifle Company. All up, there were just over 100 RAAF personnel on base, with no permanent aircraft.

The housing we were offered bordered on palatial. Where previously I had lived in groups of double-storey semi-detached houses with red-polished concrete floors in Tanjong Tokong, this time around, my wife and I lived in a three-bedroom, three-bathroom condominium with polished marble floors on the 17th floor of a 27-floor high-rise tower at No 1 Gurney Parade. The condominium had two pools, tennis courts, a gymnasium, under-cover parking, security guards and a mini-market.

The majority of my RAAF colleagues socialised with other Air Force personnel. Most had little contact with others outside of their work group. With my wife's family close by, and friends we had made at the church we joined, we spent most of our time socialising with our local friends and family. We loved eating out at the numerous restaurants and hawker stalls in and around George Town, and our friends and family members loved visiting us in our "condo".

Now, speaking of eating out, Penang is renowned for its

food. With influences as diverse as Malay, South China, Tamal Indian, Nonya and Thai, it is both delicious and appetising, hot and spicy, sour and fiery, and all-in-all mouth-watering. I have not only tried "interesting" dishes, I love some that I never would have thought I would. Trying to choose a favourite Penang dish is nigh on impossible; there are so many from which to choose. But here is a sample of those I love: char-koay-teow (a spicy noodle dish), fish-head curry, roti chanai (a pancake served with chicken curry), Hainan chicken rice, and pork rendang.

Penang was not just the birthplace of my wife, it was also where our son was born, but not as you might imagine. Sadly, we could not have children of our own. So, within weeks of arriving back on posting, my wife asked if we could adopt. It is a long story, so I will not bore you with the details, but we put out word that we wanted to adopt. Shortly after, a friend of a friend of a friend knew someone who was pregnant and did not want to keep the baby. Some weeks later, we met the parents and agreed to take the child. That was in April. Our son was born in August. We went through the Social Welfare Department and went to court and eventually the judge agreed that we could adopt him. The whole process was ridiculously simple.

In the nearly three decades that we have been back in Australia, we have visited Penang four times. Each time has been an occasion to catch up with family and friends, to eat lots of yummy food, to buy some inexpensive, good quality clothing (did I tell you that Penang is a shopper's paradise?) and to visit many of our old stomping grounds.

On our last visit, we travelled with another couple and stayed at the City Bayview Hotel which is located at the bottom of the main street in George Town, Penang Road. The rooms are a good size and the included breakfast catered for both western and oriental tastes — how would you like to try roti chanai for breakfast? The hotel is close to several banks, an assortment of hawker stalls and restaurants, and is only a short trishaw or taxi ride to a number of tourist attractions, department stores and jewellery shops.

 We hope to visit the Pearl of the Orient again next year, so long as my health holds up. And while I am looking forward to some more char-koay-teow and fish-head curry, I am sure there are new equally delicious dishes I have yet to try out.

Doors

The air was cool that morning as I waited on the platform for my train that would take me to my office in the city. I shivered as I pulled up the collar of my duffel-coat and stuck my left hand in my pocket. The temperature felt colder than it really was due to a stiff southerly breeze that was blowing. Dust, leaves and pieces of rubbish swirled around in eddies on the crowded platform. As the commuter train pulled into the station, the passengers jostled one another, trying to second-guess where the doors would stop. When the train eventually came to a standstill and the doors had opened, we all surged toward the openings. The train gorged on the passengers and in no time, the platform was empty.

In spite of the large crowd outside, it seemed that everyone found a seat once inside the carriage. After a garbled message emitted from the public address speakers, the doors closed and the train started to pull away from the station. I settled into my seat and took a newspaper from my briefcase and began to read the story on the front page; yet another scandal about another politician.

Presently, a steward moved down the aisle stopping at each passenger. As she approached my seat, I automatically reached for my ticket to show her that I was riding lawfully. So, I was mildly surprised when she asked me to place my briefcase under the seat in front and fasten my seatbelt. Since when do trains have seatbelts I wondered, as I obediently followed her instructions?

My wonder turned to consternation however, when, with a roar of its engines, the train quickly gathered speed and I was forced into the back of my seat. I looked out of the window and saw that the ground was speeding past when suddenly the train leapt into the air – we were flying!

Alarmed, I quickly glanced around at the faces of my fellow passengers. No-one else appeared in the least surprised that we were now climbing into the sky. I closed my eyes.

When I opened them again, the train was back on terra firma and coming to a stop at a station. I made a beeline for the door. I did not know where we were, but I did not care; I had to get out before the train made another aerial attempt. When the train stopped and the doors opened, I leapt onto the platform. The doors of the train closed and it sped off down the track into darkness.

I looked around and realised that I was at a station within a tunnel. No one else had alighted from the train with me and no other person was in sight. I looked left and right. Graffiti adorned the walls, but there were no other signs to say where I was or that gave directions to where I should go. At one end of the platform there was a set of stairs and at the other end an elevator. I made for the elevator. The shiny stainless-steel doors stood in stark contrast to the surroundings. I pressed the only button, which immediately glowed red.

The wait for the lift doors to open seemed interminable. Without warning and soundlessly the doors opened, gliding softly into their recesses. As I expected, the elevator was empty. I entered the small enclosure and the doors glided silently closed behind me. The mirrored walls of the elevator reflected my image back to me on all sides, including the floor and ceiling. I idly wondered how embarrassing it would be if a young woman in a short dress was in here with me.

There was light in the elevator, but not from any source that I could determine. I looked for a button to press, but there was nothing. Nothing to open or close the doors, nothing to tell it where I wanted to go, and alarmingly, no button to press or telephone to call in an emergency. Was this an emergency, I wondered?

There was no sound, but I sensed the steady gathering of speed as the elevator ascended. My legs gradually became heavier and heavier as it accelerated upwards. How high it rose, I could only guess – surely, no building could be this tall. As the elevator approached the top of its climb, it slowed dramatically – my stomach doing somersaults as the deceleration forces worked on my body. Still clutching my briefcase in a clammy hand, I waited for the doors to open. I stepped out into a dark narrow alleyway.

Although I had boarded the train after sunrise, the sky above me was now fully dark. I struggled to comprehend the passage of time. I could see very little of my immediate surrounds, but the smells of putrefying rubbish assaulted my nostrils. The sounds of the city were all around me: the dull thumping of music, screams and yelling, taxis and buses, sirens wailing and horns blaring.

All of a sudden, I felt something sharp press against my back and a gravely voice spoke into my ear, 'Gimme ya money.'

Having taken some self-defence classes the previous year, I quickly took a step forward while turning my body away from the voice and the knife. I swung my briefcase up and around catching the would-be mugger off guard, my case hitting him on the side of his jaw. His body fell limply to the ground with a thud, the blade clattering harmlessly away into a pile of garbage in the darkness. I did not wait to see if the thug was alright, but raced toward an open doorway in the hope of finding refuge. I guessed the door might be the back entrance to a restaurant or a nightclub; it was neither.

Once inside, I found another door that was closed but unlocked. I knocked, but there was no answer. I opened the heavy door and found myself in a dimly lit corridor with rows of doors on either side. The deep-pile red carpeted floor muffled the sound of my footsteps as I walked slowly to the other end. From several of the doors came the sounds of groaning and moaning. I seemed to have found myself inside a house of ill repute. I smiled at the thought that I was feeling embarrassed that I might be caught inside a brothel, a place I had not been since my buck's night, over 35 years ago.

At the far end of the corridor, a door opened and then slammed shut again followed by a man shouting and then a woman screaming. As I approached the door, I could hear slapping sounds. I was outraged at the thought that some poor defenceless young woman was being assaulted by a brute of a man, even if she was a prostitute. I burst through the door to rescue her, only to find myself in the spotlight on a stage in a theatre.

I tried to shield my eyes from the glare and stumbled over a small stool lying in my path. The crowd had erupted into cheers and applause at my arrival, which quickly turned to jeers and catcalls at my clumsy attempts at trying to find the exit. Eventually I made my way to the side of the stage where I was unceremoniously shown the door. With a shove in my back, I fell, lying sprawled in the gutter.

I did not know where I was, how I had got there, or, more importantly, how I could get to a place of safety. I sat up and reached for my phone, but it was not there, and neither was my watch or my wallet. Even my briefcase had disappeared – I must have dropped it when I fell over on the stage.

Moments later, a police paddy wagon pulled up and two officers got out whom, I thought, had come to my rescue. Without saying anything, they picked me up and threw me into the back of the police wagon. One yelled, 'Watch your fingers!' as he slammed the door shut.

'There must be a mistake,' I called, but there was no reply. I repeated my plea of innocence when we arrived at the station, but I was dragged backwards into a cell and left alone on the floor. Before I could do or say anything else, I heard the door slam shut and the bolt being slid into place. Moments later, the single light globe was extinguished.

In the dark, I felt around the cell. Behind me was a raised platform with a vinyl covered mattress, a similarly covered pillow and a single blanket. I could smell the foul stench of vomit mixed with urine. I raised myself off the floor, lay on the mattress and pulled the blanket over my body.

Suddenly I became aware of another presence in the room. 'Who's there?' I asked.

'Just an old wino,' croaked a voice.

'There's been a mistake,' I cried, 'I shouldn't be here.'

'We're all in the same boat pal,' said the voice, slurring his words. 'They bail us in the morning when we've sobered up, and then we do it all over again. At least we'll get a cooked breakfast before they kick us out.'

'But I haven't had anything to drink!' Tears welled in my eyes as I pondered my predicament. I began to sob uncontrollably.

Through his drunken haze, my companion reached out to me in a moment of compassion. 'Don't worry son,' he said consolingly, 'you'll get used to it.'

I did not want to get used to it – I should not even be here, I screamed out in my mind.

After a while, the old wino fell into a deep, alcohol-fuelled sleep. And despite the snores from my companion and the cries from another prisoner away in the darkness, I too eventually fell asleep.

The following morning, the door opened and light flooded in. I awoke and blinked for several moments, not fully comprehending my surroundings.

I vowed, 'I am never going to open or close another door ever again.'

A Life Revolving

It started a long time ago now – maybe ten or twelve years – it is difficult to remember exactly. I noticed a change in my voice. It was as if my tongue had slowed down – it could not keep up with my brain – and so I could not get the words out fast enough as I spoke. It was almost like watching one of those television programs where the actor's voice was out of sync with his lips as he spoke, only I was the actor. Nobody else noticed at first, but I knew something was not quite right.

My GP sent me to see an Ear, Nose and Throat (ENT) Specialist who diagnosed me with bowed vocal cords. He, in turn, sent me to see a Speech Pathologist. After a couple of visits, she eventually suggested that my problem was likely neurological rather than physiological. A further visit to my GP and he referred me to a Neurologist. And thus, began a six-year frustrating search for a diagnosis, all the while new and worsening symptoms appeared, affecting my speech, swallowing, balance and coordination.

I must say, at this time I was criticised by a number of people because of my "obsession" in trying to find a diagnosis. My GP told me that he had a number of patients who had symptoms similar to mine of unknown origin, while a friend from church suggested I should just "accept it". Well, I am not a fatalist and I was not prepared to accept anything, and besides, without a diagnosis, there can be no prognosis. I did not know how far or fast the condition would progress. I did not know if I would die with it or from it. And, of course, without a diagnosis, there could be no treatment.

Throughout this six-year time period, I saw numerous other specialists, including a Geneticist, and underwent literally hundreds of blood tests, countless physical examinations, CT scans, MRI scans and several painful spinal taps. All of these investigations merely ruled out what I didn't have, rather than rule in what I had. In the end, I found that I did not have spinocerebellar ataxia of genetic origin, Fredreich's Ataxia, CADASIL or MS (if you have not heard of them, ask Dr Google).

Eventually, my Neurologist sent me to another specialist, a Professor of Neurology at Westmead Hospital in Sydney. While a cynic might suggest that my Neurologist may simply have run out of ideas and given up, in practice, it turned out to be a stroke of genius. Still, it would be another 12 months and many more blood tests, scans, physical examinations and spinal taps before he came up with a hypothesis: that my condition was caused by my immune system. However, the only way the hypothesis could be tested was to start me on a course of therapy that suppressed my immune system, and to do that, he needed an Immunologist.

I first saw my Immunologist (also a Professor at Westmead Hospital) about four years ago. After examining me, he ordered yet another raft of blood tests, spinal taps and scans. Eventually, I was admitted to the hospital for a course of treatment that was followed up by a course of medication (immunosuppressants). The treatment and drugs I received is similar to that given to an organ transplant recipient or a cancer patient.

I was a pretty enthusiastic patient at first because, for the first time in eight years, I could see my symptoms improve. However, the improvements did not last, and they were soon joined by increasingly debilitating side-effects. I was soon given further drugs to treat the side-effects of the first lot of drugs. Now, I take eight tablets in the morning, and a further six tablets at night (not including complimentary medicines), as well as a further four tablets that I take on a weekly basis. A number of the drugs warn of possible adverse outcomes including things like kidney and liver failure and an over-sensitivity to the sun resulting in skin cancer. I am also very sensitive to alcohol, so I have had to drastically cut down my intake of wine and beer, not that I drank much anyway. Now, I hardly drink at all.

In time, the improvements in my symptoms slowed and eventually started to reverse. I had been treated as an in-patient on three separate occasions, and while there was an improvement spike on each occasion, these became less and less. I was also finding it increasingly difficult to be treated so far away from home, especially as my wife was, herself, not well. At last, my Immunologist suggested I start on a course of infusions of a drug that had been used as a weapon during World War 1, mustard gas, or as the drug is called, Cyclophosphamide. Unfortunately, this treatment offered up yet another set of side-effects and possible adverse outcomes, including cancer. All along I just wanted to get better – I did not want to get worse. I certainly did not want to die in the process. I mean, what is the point of curing the disease, but dying from the treatment?

Recently, I asked my Immunologist how many patients like me he was treating. Remembering he is a Professor of Immunology at one of the largest hospitals in Sydney. He replied that I was the only one. But rather than making me feel special, unique even, I suddenly felt very much alone.

Throughout my journey, the reaction of others to my neurological condition has made it even more difficult than it should otherwise have been. I have already mentioned above the comments made by my GP and my church friend. On another occasion, I was out for a walk with my wife. It was about 6:20 am and we ran into the pastor of a church we used to attend. When he heard me speak – my speech was slurred by this time – he accused me of being drunk. I was quite embarrassed.

But it is the general lack of empathy that I find most difficult to deal with. When you have a serious medical condition like cancer, chronic heart disease, leukemia, kidney disease, MS, cystic fibrosis, muscular dystrophy, or whatever, people generally have no difficulty in understanding what you must be going through, whether or not they have gone through it themselves. If you have a serious mental condition, or even something as simple as a broken limb, people generally have some understanding, and thus sympathy, if not real empathy.

However, when you have a neurological or a mental condition that no-one has ever heard of, let alone has a skerrick of understanding about, most people are ignorant at best, and dismissive at worst. They do not know about it, and by and large, they do not want to know, or care. They certainly do not care about the impact your condition has on you or your loved ones.

So, what have been the impacts? The largest by far was our fortnightly visits to Westmead Hospital for the Cyclophosphamide infusions. I never sleep well the night before, or the night after. We would wake at 3:30 am and leave home by 4:30. The infusion took anywhere from five to seven hours, and we would return home around 3:00 or 4:00 pm. It was a long day. Thankfully, I am no longer on Cyclophosphamide. However, I now have monthly infusions of another drug called Intragam and, thankfully, it is administered locally at the John Hunter Hospital.

Nevertheless, I still suffer a lack of sleep as a side-effect of one of my medications. But some things make it much worse. I am now hyper-sensitive to coffee and dark chocolate, so I do not drink coffee after lunch, or eat dark chocolate after dinner. Yet even when I am on my best behaviour and avoid "everything", some nights I just cannot sleep, or my sleeping patterns are disrupted such that I wake after as little as two hours and then I cannot get back to sleep.

I had suffered low levels of anxiety and depression for more than 25 years. My neurological condition has impacted on my mood such that I am now even more depressed. Besides medications, I find that my writing helps.

When your life revolves around regular visits to Westmead to see specialists, and monthly visits to the John Hunter, and trying to get as much sleep as you can, there are some things that fall by the wayside, like holidays – we have not had one in several years. We had planned a trip-of-a-lifetime to Alice Springs, Uluru, Darwin and Kakadu by the Ghan train from Adelaide. But we had to cancel as we could not fit it into our schedule, let alone all the drugs we would have to take with us. Not to mention the fact that my poor balance now precludes any thought of train travel. I would like to go back to Penang, but that is also on hold for the time being, if not permanently.

When you have a condition that is very rare, there are no support groups, there is no-one to talk to, to share your experiences with, to compare treatments, or for help with daily issues and problems. As I said before, life can be so very lonely. While I now have a diagnosis of sorts and I am at last receiving treatment, I still do not have a prognosis. I still do not know if I will die with it or from it. All I know is I have had enough; I do not want to play this revolving game anymore.

Which is Best: Two, Three or Four Wheels?

After a lot of soul searching, conducting a lot of research, and saving enough pennies, I recently purchased a Mazda MX-5, a sports car, although some may not think it deserves the moniker. Still, it is an open top two-seater so, as far as I am concerned, it is a sports car (others can call it what they like). It is the modern-day interpretation of the great British sports cars of the 1950s, 60s and 70s, cars like the Austin Healey, MG (A, B, C and F), Sunbeam Alpine and Triumph (TRs and Spitfires).

I once owned a Sunbeam Alpine, purchased when I served overseas in Malaysia. It would have been nice to bring it home when I was repatriated, but as much fun as it was to drive around on Penang Island, the car was in quite poor condition. The only things that held it all together was rust and bog, in equal proportions.

When my wife and I returned to Australia, all of our household finances were committed to setting up the home and, eventually, building our own house after we moved to Melbourne. Any excess went to paying for a new car. While I had ridden a motorcycle in my youth, finding the funds to getting back on two wheels had to wait. Nevertheless, I did get a motorbike or three, the last being a Yamaha XJ900. I loved that bike, but I crashed it and ended up in hospital for nearly three months (as mentioned in an earlier story).

As I think back, I now realise that the car I drove at the time mattered little when I had a motorcycle that I enjoyed to ride. When I had the XJ900, we had a small Mazda hatchback. It was a good little car but it did not excite me like the Yamaha did. My wife wrote off the Mazda 12 days before I crashed the

XJ900. Without wheels of any kind, when I eventually left hospital, we settled on a Honda Civic. Two more Hondas followed in quick succession, followed by a Holden Astra and a Mercedes C Class.

While the Mercedes was a lovely car (and by far the most expensive car I had ever owned), I still hankered for the freedom and enjoyment that only a motorcycle could provide. My wife had become ill, and I was in a stressful job. I needed an outlet; a stress reliever; I needed another bike. I bought a Yamaha FZ1 and had a ball.

More motorcycles followed, ostensibly to improve on the shortcomings of the one that proceeded it. But, in reality, I just could not be satisfied. The Yamaha gave way to a BMW K1200GT, which gave way to a Harley-Davidson Road King Classic, which gave way to a Buell Ulysses XB12X. I loved the Buell most of all, but my own health began to deteriorate, and in particular my balance. So, the Buell gave way to a three wheeled Can-Am Spyder Roaster. While the Spyder satisfied my balance issues, it was a poor substitute for a motorcycle. I eventually got rid of it. I even experimented with a classic BSA Outfit (a motorcycle with sidecar), but that was worse than the Spyder. That was when I decided to look for a sports car.

Shortly after I purchased my Mazda MX-5, a mate asked me if I thought the car was the next best thing to a motorbike. He had owned more cars and bikes than I can remember. He had also owned an Austin Healey Sprite with a Ford 1600 motor. It was a great little car and went like stink. I think he currently rides a BMW R1200R and drives a VW Golf GTi.

I replied that it is hard to compare a sports car like mine (especially as my MX-5 has a retractable hardtop rather than a soft top) with a motorbike. A fairer comparison would be to compare my car with a Toyota GT86 or Subaru BRZ. I said that I was sure that a soft top convertible would feel differently to mine, just as mine was different in feel to a motorbike. It really all boils down to personal preference.

I remember that after I bought my Spyder, I met some Spyder riders who considered that three wheels was the best thing since sliced bread. Me? I was never more than lukewarm to the Spyder. I only bought one because my poor balance precluded me from riding a motorcycle. If I could still ride a motorbike, I would probably prefer that. But since I cannot ride any more, my MX-5 is a good alternative.

In a perfect world, I would have both, a motorcycle and a sports car. But I do not.

Why?

It was one of the first questions I heard my son ask. Why dad? Why is this or that as it is. His little mind was like a sponge, soaking up all manner of information, details and facts as he grew. I never fobbed him off and always gave him an answer, even if it was, I really do not know. But in time, after he graduated to high school and then to university, he stopped asking. I think it was because he thought I could no longer answer his questions.

However, recently, I heard the question again. Only this time it was my wife asking why, and it was about me. Of all your siblings, she asked, why is it only you that has been struck down with this neurological condition? It is a question I have been asking myself all my life. Why was I the only one to have juvenile asthma? Why was I the only one to have eye problems necessitating the wearing of glasses? Why were my wife and I the only ones in our family unable to conceive and have children naturally? Why was I forced to retire due to poor health? And yes, why did I come down with a neurological condition, when there was no family history of such? It is a series of questions we had no answers for.

Now, before my Christian friends reply, what about Romans 8:28, *"And we know that for those who love God all things work together for good, for those who are called according to his purpose."* (ESV) Well yes, I know this verse as well as anyone, and it has been a sore testing of my faith to continue trusting God that this was true. But what is the good that can come out of these happenings, these illnesses, these health problems. Yes, I know God is sovereign and has control of all things, but how is this or that condition or illness or tragic circumstance working out for my good?

More to the point, how then, as members of a congregation, or fellowship of believers, how do you or I minister to someone who has just received bad news about themselves or one of their family members? To use the verse above as a weapon to test their faith is glib, at best. At worst, it is cruel and unfair, and in the end, it can be very discouraging and disheartening.

So, what do you say to a young couple who wake to find their infant has succumbed to SIDS? What do you say to a young father whose teenage son has been diagnosed with brain cancer? What do you say when a young mother is told she has only months to live due to an aggressive form of breast cancer? They want to know why. Why them? Why now?

Of course, we know that all illnesses and death are the result of sin and the Fall of Genesis 3. But to suggest this to someone who is grieving the loss of a loved one or who has a serious health issue is also very unfair. I remember a comment by a person from church about my wife's psychological condition and whether sin was involved. I found it very upsetting at the time.

It is like the question the disciples asked the Lord Jesus when they found a man born blind. They asked him, *"who sinned, this man or his parents?"* Jesus replied that it was neither, *"but that the works of God might be displayed in him."* (John 9:2-3) Yes, sin was the ultimate culprit, but there was also a more important issue in this case. Jesus healing of the blind man showed that he, Jesus, was the one to overcome the consequences of the Fall.

But of course, this is not the answer to all cases of illness. Jesus does not suddenly appear and heal everyone who needs healing. God can and does heal, but he doesn't always, as the Apostle Paul discovered. But he also discovered that God's grace was all sufficient. (2 Corinthians 12:7-10)

Several years ago, I purchased a book by Rev D.A. Carson called, *How Long, O Lord? Reflections on suffering and evil*. It is a great book and I highly recommend it to anyone who is going through health difficulties, grieving, or to those who might be ministering to them. Near the end of the book, he writes:

> Frequently in the midst of suffering the most comforting "answers" are simple presence, help, silence, tears. Helping with the gardening or preparing a casserole may be far more spiritual an exercise than the exposition of Romans 8:28. The Scriptures themselves exhort us to mourn with those who mourn (Rom. 12:15).

Furthermore, as someone who has been there, done that, and who has the scars to prove it, I am as well qualified to help a brother or sister in Christ who has just been diagnosed with a serious illness, or whose spouse or child has a serious health problem, to get through a difficult period. Not that I have all the answers, mind you. But I understand how they might be feeling, I can pray with and for them, and encourage them to continue trusting that God does indeed work all things for good.

Maybe this is the real answer to the question why!

THE END

Endnotes:

[i] First published in *Yarns Down the Track*, 2018, Stroud Writers FAW
[ii] First published in *High Heels & Hobnail Boots*, 2013, Stroud Writers FAW
[iii] First published in *Yarns Down the Track*, 2018, Stroud Writers FAW
[iv] First published in *Penang Monthly*, February 2019 issue 02.19, Penang Institute.

Printed in Great Britain
by Amazon